Ask the Narcissist.

The Answers to Your Questions

By

H G Tudor

Ask the Narcissist:
The Answers to Your Questions

By

H G Tudor

Published by Insight Books

Introduction

My kind are fascinating creatures. Held in revulsion and awe, the narcissist is a person who has a significant impact on everyone he or she interacts with. People are lifted up, people are used, people are treated like kings and queens, people are loved with an intensity they have never experienced and people are abused in horrendous ways. People are manipulated, people are confused, people are exploited, people are made to feel wonderful, people are drained and discarded. The stark contrast that exists between being treated like a god and then cast down into the dirt below confuses and bewilders. Those who have experienced the effects of being ensnared by a narcissist will never be free of the effects of this engagement. They may restore their sanity, rescue their finances, the bruises will heal and the anxiety recedes. No contact may be instigated and maintained to minimize the allure of the narcissist. The memories may begin to lessen over time and their addictive quality fade a degree, through a combination of the passage of time and the resolute determined discipline of the victim to keep the narcissist from out of his or her mind. The ever presence that we have installed in our victims may lose some of its potency given time and technique but there is one issue which always threatens to draw a victim back into our grasp. Unanswered questions.

The behaviour of the narcissist often makes no sense to normal and healthy people because they look at the world through their eyes and not those of the narcissist. The things we say and do appear beyond comprehension. We govern our kingdoms through the application of confusion and illogical behaviour. What many people fail to grasp is that our behaviour is entirely logical to us. It makes perfect sense when looked at through our eyes. If people were able to put themselves in our places, then they would have a much better opportunity to make sense of why we do as we do. They may not accept what we do as right, they may find it abhorrent but they will at least gain an understanding as to why we engage in this behaviour. By achieving understanding the victim will go a long way to enabling themselves to recover, guard against future incursions by our kind and ultimately achieve freedom. So often a victim will still feel a compulsion to contact, be with and engage again with the narcissist even though the victim knows what this person has done to them and is capable of doing so again. Intelligent, sensible and independent individuals will place themselves in the line of fire once more because they need to receive answers to the many questions that the narcissist has left them with.

This unfinished business is a typical maneuver undertaken by our kind to allow us a route back into your life. As an empathic individual, you have a desire to know and understand. This burns away inside and prevents you from gaining closure after your encounter with us and instead compels you to want to become exposed to us once again. These questions run round and round in your minds, causing you upset, confusion and anguish until you contact your tormentor in the hope, albeit a vain and misplaced one, of getting answers. We know you want to do this. We rely on you doing this to allow us to hoover you back into our fantasy world once more and recommence the narcissistic cycle and drink deep of your delicious hoover fuel.

Often the narcissist you have engaged with will not provide you with any answers. This is because he or she does not know what they are and therefore cannot be in any position to explain themselves in a manner which makes sense to you and is satisfactory. Furthermore, even if we do know and have the answers, we will provide you with tit bits in order to maintain your interest and keep you exposed to us so we can keep gaining fuel from you. We will promise the provision of answers whilst giving you some morsel to consider but we will never satisfy your appetite for answers.

This book changes that situation. All of my writings provide you with explanations and answers to why we say and do certain things in the progression of the relationship with our kind. From the outset of targeting you through to a hoover, I have detailed much by way of clarification and explanation and that work continues and is ongoing as part of my treatment as I gain a greater understanding of what I am, in order to pass this information to those who choose to read my works. Those publications will expand on many different points and through reading them you will enhance your understanding and increase your chances of achieving freedom. This book aims to respond to some of the most commonly asked questions of people like me. It is a collection of those questions which I have often been asked by my victims and also questions that contributors have provided in order to seek answers for themselves. I have collated fifty questions which represent a broad selection of queries arising out of the engagement with our kind. From seduction, to devaluation, from targeting to discard and from hoovering to abusing, all areas have been addressed. These answers are given in a direct and understandable fashion. There is no long-winded scientific discourse here, but rather hard-hitting and at times uncomfortable truths. However, as I often explain, the best medicine usually tastes the worst. Accordingly, in order to allow you the best chance to recover from your entanglement with the narcissist and avoid the detrimental effects of dealing with unfinished business and outstanding questions, this publication will provide you with an unrivalled access to information and knowledge, direct from the mind of the narcissist. Use it well and have your questions answered. I have indicated at appropriate junctures where further reading can be found on certain subjects. Of course, if these fifty questions do not include ones that you have, do contact me (details at the end of the book) and pose them.

1.Why do you sometimes ignore our compliments? (From Hope)

We ordinarily love to be complimented. Praise, admiration and adoration can all be exhibited through the provision of a compliment. If you compliment our new tie, our car, our hair cut, our politeness or our compliments which we lavish on you, you are providing us with fuel. The words combined with the emotion gives us the positive fuel which we want from you during our seduction of you. Compliments and flattery are very important to us. During the seduction period, this is what we want from you. We want it each and every day and frequently. Given that this is so important to us why then would we ever ignore a compliment?

We do this when we are devaluing you. As an honest and decent person you know that passing a compliment about someone is a good and pleasant thing to do. The recipient will feel good. He or she will smile and thank you, possibly return the compliment or shrug with embarrassed modesty. This person will not ignore what you have just said. We ignore it in order to gain negative fuel from you and to confuse you. Ignoring you in any event is ill-mannered and rude. To do so when you are paying us a compliment is even worse. In all likelihood this will create a reaction from you of irritation or upset and accordingly this amounts to negative fuel. This also confuses you because you cannot understand why, once upon a time, we reveled in your compliments and also why would anyone ever ignore being complimented? You do not understand why we do this and your confusion is likely to lead you to ask us what is wrong, what have you done and so forth. These questions will be invariably asked in an urgent and pleading manner which provides us with additional negative fuel. Thus, ignoring your compliments is a manipulative technique for the purposes of drawing fuel from you and also creating confusion and consequently exerting further control over you.

2.Do you fool everyone or only those closest to you? (From Susan)

We aim to fool everyone that we come into contact with. Those people who form our secondary and tertiary sources are usually left in a lengthy period of seduction, except for when they become disloyal, question us, fail to carry out what we want and most of all, fail to supply us with fuel. Many people can remain as these sources, without ever suffering our devaluation. Accordingly, since they only ever know our charming and magnetic side, they are fooled all of the time. It is rare for us to commence our engagement with somebody by way of devaluation (although it may happen with a stranger, remote stranger and/or minion for the purpose of gaining negative fuel or triangulating with a superior source by putting down the minion to gain the admiration of a new prospect). Instead, we expose these fuel sources to our charm, brilliance, kindness and generosity and in turn we fool them all. They form part of our façade and their fooling continues. There may be the occasional person who is not fooled by us. Usually, we recognize that they will not be prove a fruitful and reliable source of fuel first so we do not target that person. Once in a while, we may not realize and we may target somebody who sees the red flags (even if they do not know what we truly are) and therefore they realize something is wrong and move away from our grasp. In other instances, the target may prove to be someone who is one of our kind or exhibits strong traits of our kind and therefore will not be a useful source of fuel. They may not realize we have established this, but we do not fool them by choice.

Naturally, we save our most effective manipulations for fooling those who we allow to become closest to us, because these individuals provide us with the best fuel, regularly and reliably. Accordingly, we always fool these individuals in order to secure our fuel.

3.Why can't you stop texting other women? Or just admit that you do it and admit that you don't want to stop? (From E)

Technology has furthered our reach like nothing before. It allows us to cast our snaking tendrils far and wide. It allows us to reach more people over greater distances and with such regularity that it provides us with a fantastic medium by which to seduce, devalue, discard and hoover. The text message ranks amongst the best way of using this technological advantage. There are several reasons why we cannot stop texting other women.

a. They are providing us with fuel. We are charming them and seducing them and this causes them to respond with admiring and adoring texts which provides us with fuel;
b. It allows a quick and easy way of receiving fuel, from multiple sources;
c. It allows us to seduce these other women as we use them as secondary sources of fuel or possibly to tee them up to replace you as the primary source of fuel;
d. We know it upsets and irritates you. By triangulating you with these other women through the use of text messages we are able to draw negative fuel from you;
e. This triangulation causes you to be aware that there is a potential threat to your status as primary source (although you do not realise you are the primary source, you will regard it as a threat to your position as our intimate partner) and therefore you will try harder to cling on to us, please us and/or do what we want;

In terms of why will we not admit it (even though it is obvious what we are doing), we will not admit it as if we did so we allow the following to happen: -

a There is the potential loss of your negative fuel because you are not reacting to us doing this as a consequence of having detected what we are doing and gaining an admission from us;

b.   We are never wrong;

c.   By denying it this provides us with an opportunity to blame you, provoke you and thus draw more negative fuel;

d.   You will feel like you have gained the upper hand, even if it is momentary, by obtaining this admission. We do not like any shift in power to you, however fleeting.

e.   This will feel like a criticism to us and we hate to be criticised.

It is correct that we do not want to stop because we cannot stop. We need to gather fuel and this is an efficient and effective way of doing so. For the reasons advanced above, we will not admit that we do not want to stop either.

4.Why do you find it so easy to move straight from one relationship into another? (From So Sad)

It is entirely correct that we move with frightening and bewildering ease from one relationship to another. This is applicable to many of our relationships; friends, colleagues and so forth but it is most relevant to the intimate relationship. This is because ordinarily there is a gap between intimate relationships and because this swift transition from one intimate relationship to another causes considerable upset and harm. There are several reasons why we find it so easy: -

a. We are not hampered or hindered by considerations such as guilt, regret, compassion or remorse. Normal people are affected by these emotions and considerations which mean that they conduct themselves in a different fashion when being in a relationship, ending that relationship and entering a new one;

b. Our need for fuel overrides any other considerations. If our current intimate partner is no longer providing us with premium negative fuel through the devaluation, because they are numbed to the point of barely functioning through our behavior or because they know what we are doing, then they are of no use to us. We do not care that this person has loved us, treated us well, housed us, supported us, provided us with money and so forth. All of those considerations become irrelevant compared to the ability of that person to provide us with fuel. Thus, they must be cast aside. The need for fuel means we have to move on to somebody straight away and in all likelihood we will have been drawing fuel from someone else prior to your discard which is a further reason why we move on so quick.

c. We have somebody already lined up. The provision of fuel must be unbroken and consequently we will have seduced someone else and we will have them waiting in the wings, already providing us with fuel, ready to replace the current incumbent.

d. We are experts at charming people and therefore we find it very easy to secure a new intimate partner. Who would not want to be our intimate partner when you are subjected to our love-bombing seduction and our golden period?

e. Our dislike of you for failing us in the provision of fuel propels our seduction of the new person. Thus what has gone before powers that which is to come;

f. We can jettison thoughts and memories of you once you have been discarded and we rarely think of you again because we are so pre-occupied with our new target (and those who will ultimately replace that new target) so there is next to no "drag effect" caused by lingering memories of you;

g. The fact we chose you and you let us down disgusts us and in order to eradicate that sensation we need someone new, someone not like you, someone better and brighter. This again drives us into a new relationship very quickly;

Accordingly, there are many reasons why we move into a new relationship so readily. We have to do so for the reason of gaining fuel and we are not hampered by the usual concerns that somebody normal would have about the end of one relationship and the entering of another.

5. How do you choose your victim? (From Erica)

Our victims are chosen as a consequence of a two stage process. We frequent Hunting Grounds which are environments where there will be a higher frequency of targets who have the traits which are most attractive to us, dependent on the type of narcissist that we are. For example, A Somatic Narcissist who is driven by physical appearance and attractiveness, material possessions and physical prowess uses hunting grounds such as night clubs and gyms. The methodology that we apply is to undertake background checks on our target. We will observe the target, question that person's friends and family, use our Lieutenants to obtain information from them and obtain them and scour that person's online presence for information. This information will confirm (or deny) that the proposed target is viable for us and will also provide us with intelligence which can then be used in the forthcoming seduction to maximize its prospects of success. Once the background checks have been undertaken then we engage with the target to confirm that he or she is a viable target and look for the green lights which confirm that our seduction is likely to meet with success. This combination of remote background checks and personal engagement provides us with sufficient information to ascertain whether you have the traits which we value and then with the means by which we can commence a successful seduction.

6. Do you sleep well at night? (From Angela)

Yes, I do. I fall asleep promptly and wake ready for a new day of gathering fuel with revitalized energy levels. I am not hindered by conscience, regret or guilt, such things which are designed to keep people awake at night. I ensure that my planning and machinations have been concluded for the day before I retire. I ensure I have received sufficient fuel to feel calm and at ease and without being troubled by remorse for the things that I have done during the day (as judged by people who are built a different way from me) I sleep the sleep of the righteous.

By contrast we like to disrupt your sleep and have you in a near permanent state of tiredness. This means that our manipulative behavior becomes magnified. You are too tired to fight back; you lose control of your emotions more readily which in turn provides us with fuel. You begin to doubt yourself and confined yourself to the essentials, namely house and work, forgoing social activities and hobbies which makes it easier for us to exert our hold over you. We will make you stay up late, arrange for you to be woken early and prevent you from napping during the day if possible in order to maintain this state of fatigue.

7. Why are you so angry and so often? (From Sophie)

We are not angry. Angry is a normal and understandable emotion which normal and healthy people experience. We experience fury. It is always with us, churning away beneath the surface as a consequence of our hatred of the injustices which the world has delivered against us. This fury surfaces by reason of ignition. You invariably cause this ignition because you criticize us. We hate to be criticised. We cannot stand it at all. Your criticism will be either real or more often perceived by us. We find such criticism in many things. Being ignored is a criticism, not asking our view is criticism, serving us after someone else is a criticism. Such is our elevated view of ourselves, our innate superiority and god-like status, we cannot bear to experience anything that suggests we are anything but superior and god-like. Accordingly, should this happen we experience criticism and this ignites our fury. If you bring us the wrong type of spanner when we are working on a car, if you cook something we do not fancy eating even though we may have told you earlier that we wanted it or you fail to comment on a new tie we have purchased, we will regard this a criticism. We may appear to be hyper sensitive to you but we need praise and compliments and the failure to provide this does not equate to neutrality or indifference in our eyes. No, we regard indifference as criticism and our fury ignites with various consequences for you. You may think we are often angry. It goes beyond this. We are filled with a deep-seated fury and that is what you unleash when you criticize us, be it deliberate (and fuel-free) or inadvertent. To understand more on this subject, you may wish to consider **Fury.**

8. Why tell your partner you love them when you obviously don't? (From Freedom)

The words "I love you" are used regularly by our kind, indeed, we utter this phrase in a way that is akin to the way that others say "hello". They are said within hours of us meeting our next victim, they are said often by word, text and letter. We say it to you when we wake, when we hold you, when we make love to you and when we telephone you mid-afternoon. Our use of this phrase is extensive and we use it with everyone we identify as a prospective primary source. Why do we use it?

a. Our victims are love devotees. We identify this as a trait when we target him or her. The victim believes in the power of love and wants to love and be loved. Telling this person that we love them taps into this deep-seated desire of the victim;

b. It provides a connection between us and the victim and does so at an early stage;

c. Combined with our other methods of love-bombing, the fact that you have been told that someone as wonderful and as magnificent as me proves extremely difficult to resist. Who would not want to be loved in such a way?

d. We say it to you to cause you to fall in love with us. By telling you that we love you, we are paving the way for you to reciprocate. You want to fall in love and you want someone like us (because we are mirroring all the things you like) and the fact we have said it first creates a "safe" environment for you to tell us. The difference is of course being that you mean it;

e. By telling you we love you, you will respond in a similar fashion and this provides us with fuel;

f. We tell you that we love you to create something (even though it is false) to take away from you when we devalue you and to have the maximum impact on you for provoking the provision of negative fuel;

g. What we are actually telling you is that we love your fuel because that is what we actually love;

h. We are able to say it even though we do not feel it because we know how to mimic appearing in love because we have seen it so many times and we are experts at mimicry. We are not burdened by any sense of guilt or regret at behaving this way. All we want is your fuel.

9. If we break up with you, why do you need to have the "last word" and pretend you are the ones who are done with us? (From Hope)

This is a consequence of our belief in our superiority and the need to maintain this superiority. We regard you as inferior to us. You are blessed to be allowed into our presence and you have benefitted from our kindness, our generosity, our humour, our largesse and so forth during the golden period. You then failed to continue to provide us with the positive fuel despite the fact that we gave you so much. This failure underlines your inferiority and this is what we drive at you and reinforce during devaluation. We cannot allow somebody who is inferior to have any say or determination over what we are and what we do. Accordingly, should you end the relationship with us, this is a criticism of us. You are suggesting that we are unimportant and indeed, we are unimportant compared to you, a person who is inferior. This is a massive insult. This ignites our fury and one of the ways this manifests is our need to have the last word. This last word means that we assert our superiority. We are "doing" we are not "done to". By having the last word, we maintain our superiority and this allows us to repair the damage done to us through your criticism. This last word may mean that we have discarded you (in our minds at least) or that we will now subject you to a silent period (the relationship is not actually over in our minds, but we have "won" the last battle) before we return and act as if nothing has happened as we hoover you.

10. If you instigate no contact against us are you waiting for us to go banging on your door or to shoot you some sappy email telling them how sorry we are, and how horrible we treated them? If you love negative fuel how is that you block us when we call them out? My narcissist said to me that he was done communicating with me and "let's be friends", what does he mean by that? Is that a Grand Hoover? (From Art girl)

We do not do no contact. We do a silent treatment and that is what you are getting. Yes, he expects you to go crawling to him, hammering on the door, repeatedly ringing and firing off the e-mails in order to harvest negative fuel from you. He does not regard your relationship as at an end. You may have decided it is over but he has not. Note your comment, "he was done communicating with me" – he foreshadowed your silent treatment. He will be gathering fuel elsewhere at present but he does not consider you and him to be over. He is waiting for you to go to him. If you do not do so, he will appear at some point and act as if nothing has happened. There has been no hoover because the relationship is not over, you are just in a fairly long silent treatment. The "let's be friends" line was to test what your reaction would be. If you baulked at that and got upset, he gains fuel. If you agree he knows he has an easy conduit to hoovering, you.

11. How old were you when you realized you were special? Who told you that you were special? Were you overpraised or abused as a child? (From Susan)

In retrospect, based on the comments of others, I think I have always regarded myself as special from an early age. I do recall a specific moment when I realized that I special. It was when I was aged 18 and I received my 'A' level results at Sixth Form College securing my place at a top university in the United Kingdom. My results were exceptional and my tutors told me that I had attained the highest exam results in two examining boards across the whole country. I was truly number one. That outcome combined with the fruits of my machinations over the summer between sixth form and university showed me that I was indeed special. My mother told me that I was special. It is often the case with our kind that being told we are special by one or both parents, or being treated as a special case (thus suggesting we lack being special and we are prejudiced against) is a common theme in our backgrounds.

My special status is based on considerable ability, as it is with many of our kind. Brilliant athletes, charismatic politicians and leaders, talented writers, artists and musicians, successful business people and similar form our ranks. There is always a tendency for us to embellish our success and some of our kind do it more than others, relying on very little to go a very long way. We all make use of exaggeration and we all make use of taking traits from other people to increase our attractiveness. The scope and extent of this does vary but it is always there. I was not overpraised. I was set high standards and expected to achieve and when I did achieve those standards I was rightly praised but I had to work extremely hard to earn it. If I failed, I certainly knew about it. I did not regard what was done to me as abusive but rather the consequence of either succeeding or failing and it was done for my own good. I should imagine that there are those with a particular agenda who would look at what I experienced during my childhood and regard it as abuse. As with most things, it is a question of perspective.

12 Is there anything in life you enjoy for enjoyment's sake which does not involve obtaining fuel? I know you enjoy writing but you gather fuel from this and most sports you would also obtain fuel from by playing to win but would you enjoy just lying on the beach and watching the sunset (on your own) or perhaps fishing just for relaxation? Would you watch a TV programme because you enjoyed it? Without it needing to lead to fuel in some way by perhaps impressing your new supply or upsetting an existing one? (From Alexis)

Yes, there are many things which I enjoy doing which do not involve the extraction of fuel. You mention that my writing gathers fuel but when I am sat at my keyboard with some music playing I am not gathering fuel in that moment. Admittedly, I am buoyed by thoughts of the fuel to come and I cannot deny that one of the eventual outcomes from the writing is the provision of fuel, but in that moment of the words forming in my mind and my fingers gliding across the keyboard there is no fuel and I am enjoying what I am doing. I do not watch much television other than live sport, the news and the occasional quality drama. Much of the output on television is rubbish which is served up to keep the masses docile and drooling and I detest that. I prefer to watch films, sometimes alone, often with someone else so that I can pass erudite comment at certain points during and always after, the film, to draw fuel. When alone of course I do not draw any fuel as I watch the film. I am not a fan of fishing although I have done it. I enjoy shooting (targets and clay pigeon, nothing living) and often do that effectively on my own (there is someone operating the machine but they are some distance away). I enjoy reading (when time permits) and that is very much a singular activity. I also enjoy visiting stately homes and castles, sometimes accompanied and sometimes not. I am perfectly capable of gaining enjoyment from pursuing certain activities alone but I must put this in context. The ability to do this arises from being sufficiently fueled beforehand. If I am not, I must seek out the fuel before I can engage in the pursuit or combine the two. Once I have fuel to the degree I require I can engage in the relevant pursuit alone until such time as the need for fuel arises again. It is important to understand this context in terms of me enjoying doing things that do not in themselves provide fuel.

13. Why aren't your endless complaints about me enough for you to end things and move on? (From E)

The reason I have to make endless complaints about you is because this arises from your failure to provide me with what I want. If you did this in a reliable and consistent fashion, then I would have no reason to complain about you. If you kept supplying me with the positive fuel that I need in a regular manner and of the necessary potency I would not have to complain. You fail to do so and you let me down. Accordingly, you cause me to complain. This is done to punish you for your failure and also to make you respond in a way that provides me with negative fuel. This means that you will become angry, frustrated and/or upset and in turn give me the negative fuel which is compensation for the loss of the once potent positive fuel. I have no desire to move on when you are giving me such high quality negative fuel. That is why I continue to complain so that you will react and I will keep receiving the negative fuel. Once you diminish the provision of that negative fuel, either through your conscious decision to stop reacting in an emotional fashion or the level of abuse is such that you start to shut down and fail to respond as a last ditch defence mechanism, then you will cause me to look elsewhere for the fuel from a fresh primary source. I will though be back at some point to gain some hoover fuel.

14.. Do you ever feel genuine remorse, even briefly, when you see someone who loves you suffering, trying to understand why you're treating them that way? (From Megan)

No I do not feel genuine remorse. I may only show a false, learned remorse during the seduction period in order to draw positive fuel from you as a consequence of your reaction to my mimicked response and also to keep you bound to me and drawn closer. This false remorse will also appear as part of a hoover (Respite, Initial Grand, Benign Follow-Up – **See Black Hole: The Narcissistic Hoover or A Grimoire of Narcissism** for more on those types of hoovers). During devaluation you will see no remorse whatsoever. This is for the simple reason that we do not feel it. We may show it when it suits our purposes to gain fuel and exert control or manipulate. We are unable to feel remorse. This is because during the creation of what we are, remorse would not serve any purpose. It would slow us down and distract us from our primary goal which is that of obtaining fuel. In the same way that an airplane does not have huge billboards on the wings because they would affect its aerodynamics, we do not feel remorse because all it would do would be to hinder our pursuit of fuel. This would risk affecting our existence and therefore cannot be allowed. Accordingly, we never developed the capability to feel remorse. This goes for such emotions as happiness (in the sense by which you know it), joy, guilt, sympathy, empathy and regret, to name but a few. The fact that someone who loves us and is in pain does not cause us to feel remorse in the same way it might if it were you looking on. All we feel is contempt for the individual, an annoyance that we are attached to someone so pitiful but then also a contradiction which irritates all the more as we revel in the negative fuel that you provide to us. This is why such abusive cycles become self-perpetuating.

We need the negative fuel. This causes us to hurt you and provoke you to provide it. We gain the negative fuel. At the same time your response annoys us because we regard it as weak and pathetic. We then become irritated because we have to endure this in order to gain our negative fuel. This annoys us further that we are chained to someone so pathetic and therefore we lash out at you again in order to try to diminish our annoyance. It may work for a short time and you provide more negative fuel, but then the cycle starts again.

15. Why is sex important? (From Shivali)

Sex is important to us for several reasons.

a. We are (save for the Victim Narcissist) very good at it. The Cerebral Narcissist talks a good game and has sex with your mind whilst Somatic and Elite Narcissists are sexual Olympians and have a lot of experience in between the sheets which allows them to become extremely proficient;

b. Sex is a major part of the means of seduction. It is an integral part of most relationships and is often regarded as a fundamental means of expressing love for another. Our victims' statuses as love devotees means that the entwinement of sex and love makes them vulnerable to sex being used as a weapon of seduction;

c. The provision of a lot of sex during the seduction period is addictive and very pleasant;

d. The provision of a lot of sex during the seduction period creates something which can then be withdrawn during devaluation which provokes the provision of negative fuel;

e. Sex is also used as a weapon during devaluation by reducing the victim to the status of an object which the narcissist uses for his own gratification. The victim may also be forced into humiliating and degrading sex acts which increases the negative fuel for the narcissist and also provides him or her with a further means of control.

The relationship between the narcissist and sexual activity is a fascinating and wide-ranging one and you can find considerable detail and insight in **Sex and the Narcissist.**

15 Why do you lie when truth would serve you better. Why lie about the obvious? Why protect the lie when there are no negative consequences to owning up? (From Lina)

Our kind lie as easily and as readily as you draw breath. Lies serve all manner of purposes for us. They enable us to seduce, they enable us to paint a grander picture of ourselves than is the reality, they are used to confuse and control. Much of what we say is based on lies. We lie because the spoken word is so easy to use and we prefer to use it rather than take actions which require the use of our energies. Lies are a moment on our lips and the consequences can be far-reaching and advantageous for us. Dealing with the specific questions above.

The question of whether the truth or a lie will serve us better is a matter of perspective. I make mention of perspective and world views often in my work. We look at the world in a different way to you. This is why you think that our behavior makes no sense when judged on your standards, but it makes perfect stance when viewed from our perspective. This is another example of that. You regard the truth as something that would serve us better for two reasons. Firstly, this is your world view that you are seeking to impose on us. Secondly, you are, generally speaker, great believers in the truth and the need to seek the truth as part of your empathic qualities. This means that you tell the truth, want to know the truth and expect other people to exhibit the truth when dealing with you. You consider the truth to be above all else and that the truth always serves people in a better way. We disagree. The lie actually serves us better because from our perspective it achieves an outcome that we want. That outcome is usually two fold; to confuse you and to draw fuel from you. You think that if we tell the truth then the outcome will be better and therefore surely we can also see this, so we should tell the truth. You however find our need to lie bewildering (based on your standards) and our reliance on telling lies has you confused. This suits us. You are also likely to react in a frustrated fashion, become angry or be upset and any of these reactions and more beside, provide us with fuel. You also must consider that with the lesser functioning of our brethren that they actually regard what they are saying to be the truth and therefore they cannot understand why you remain so adamant that something else is the truth. You remain confused and upset and this again provides fuel.

Why do we lie about the obvious? Again, it is obvious when looked at from your perspective but from our perspective the obvious thing is to draw fuel from you and have you confused. Therefore, the outcome more than justifies the means. Again, with the lesser functioning of our kind it may not even be obvious to them, even if it is to you.

Finally, why do we protect the lie when there are no consequences to telling the truth. Once again you make this assumption based on your world view. To us there are consequences of telling the truth, namely the loss of fuel and the loss of creating confusion and thus controlling you. Those are very real consequences to us and this means that we must protect the lie in such circumstances.

Much of understanding why we lie comes down to the need to draw fuel from you, the need to control you and the fact that this governs our perspective which is entirely different to yours.

16. How can my narcissist go on posting love quotes when she clearly does not know love?

Very easily. The fact that we do not feel love in the same way as you do not amount to a bar to us using love as a weapon. As mentioned above, one of your empathic qualities is being a love devotee and this adherence to love and all that is associated with it makes you vulnerable and susceptible to love being used against you. We are adept at using loving literature, poems, quotes and the like to further our seduction, make a devaluation even harsher or for the purposes of a hoover. This is entirely by design and focuses in on your vulnerability. Just because we do not feel love in the way that you do, does not prohibit us from realizing just how significant it is to you, how much you want and how much you rely on it. Using love for the purposes of control and the extraction of fuel is fair game to us.

As mentioned above, since we are not hampered by feelings such as guilt, regret and remorse, using love in this way, which you would regard as a wrong use and a method of defiling love does not bother us. We do not have a conscience that will be offended by denigrating love in such a fashion. We do indeed give love a bad name. The use of the quotes as you mention will not cause your narcissist any concern. She will not have her conscience pricked and think, "Realistically I cannot rely on these quotes because I do not feel love." She will use them to ensnare you, control you and draw fuel from you because that is all that matters to her.

The use of love quotes, literature and poems is a particular red flag to be aware of during seduction. We do not feel it therefore we need to have other people provide it for us and what better way than to take the words of a romantic poet and use them for our purposes, with our without attributing them to the source.

17. Don't narcissists find it odd they fall in love with so many people? (From Cara)

Not at all. We are wonderful people. Knowledgeable, charismatic, attractive, beautiful and mesmerizing. It is not odd at all that we fall in love with so many people. In fact, it is odd that we do not fall in love with more since we are given more chances than an ordinary person. We have so many suitors, so many admirers and we are exposed to more people than usual whom we might fall in love with (owing to our attendance in the Hunting Grounds).

We do not find it odd because falling in love (our love as opposed to your concept of love) is integral to the gathering of fuel. We must fall in love with a target to enable us to give that target our all. Our complete and total love-bombing so we can ensure that the target falls in love with us (your love, not ours), becomes bound to us and most of all so that the target starts to provide us with delicious, potent and reliable streams of fuel. This is why we fall in love. This is what we do.

When that fuel becomes stale because you let us down we are driven to find a new fresh source as we berate you for your failures. As we draw negative fuel from you we are searching out those targets who will be the new hope, the new source, our new love. Thus in order to draw the positive fuel from this new target we fall in love again. It cannot be helped because this is what has to be done to seduce you, to draw you to us and to gather that fuel. If twenty people have let us down, despite our hopes that they would not do so, then we will fall in love with twenty-one people and more into the future if the need arises. We see nothing odd about this.

There is a further factor which means that it does not seem odd to us. The fact that when we find the new prospect we effectively delete you from our minds. We do not waste any time thinking about what we once did with you because it serves no purposes going forward. Admittedly, there might be the occasional reminder of you as a past appliance but the recollection will be brief as we cast it to one side. You see we recognize what memories are. They are a fleeting reminder which surfaces in one's mind, it appears and then leaves. If you let it. The only reason a memory remains in your mind and goes around and around is if you cause it to do so by thinking about it, analyzing it and giving it life and energy. We do not do that because it serves us with no purpose and enables us jettison memories when they occasionally do appear. We are too busy and too focused on the new prospect that we do not allow past memories to appear very often and if they do, they are soon dispensed with. You on the other hand allow yourself to be subsumed by memories. We do not dislike that, indeed we prefer it as it makes you vulnerable to our further manipulations, especially the hoover. We delete you form our minds and move on to the next love. Thus in our minds we do not fall in love repeatedly but we are only ever in love with one person, one appliance.

18. How many types of narcissists are there? (From So Sad) You sometimes refer to the "lesser" of your kind. Can you describe the varying degrees? (From Unpath)

Narcissists are drawn from three schools and four cadres. The schools are those of the Lesser, Mid-Range and the Greater (also known as the malign) narcissist. Briefly, the Lesser Narcissist does not have high energy levels and is of a lower functioning nature in terms of intelligence and guile. The Greater Narcissist is driven by malice, is scheming, intelligent and has significant energy reserves which drive him or her. The Mid-Range Narcissist falls between these two and is usually identified by omission, i.e. he or she does not exhibit the traits of either the Lesser or Greater Schools and thus must be Mid-Range.

In terms of the cadres, there are Victim Narcissists who use their illness, infirmity and need for mothering and care as the principle means by which they ensnare their prey. Somatic Narcissists are motivated by physical attractiveness, physical prowess, material items and symbols of status. The Cerebral Narcissist exhibits significant intellectual capabilities and uses his or her power of their mind to lure in their victims. They are not especially bothered by appearances although that does not mean that they necessarily neglect their own but rather the more "noble" pursuits of knowledge, art and literature are of greater importance. The Elite Narcissist contains the traits of both Somatic and Cerebral Narcissists creating someone who is both appealing to look at and is in possession of a great mind. There are those which may be largely Somatic with occasional Cerebral features and vice versa as the cadres do bleed into one another.

The schools apply to the cadres, so one can find a Greater Elite Narcissist but not all of the schools are applicable, accordingly one does not find a Lesser Cerebral

Narcissist. Each of these types and the requisite combinations are driven by different traits which they find desirable in their victims. They look for certain indicators when undertaking their targeting and back ground checks. The differing categories of narcissist also conduct themselves in different ways in terms of their methods of seduction, devaluation and hoovering, although there are many similarities between them also. For further detailed information on this you can read more in **Sitting Target: How and Why the Narcissist Chooses You.**

19 Why can't I get closure with a narcissist? Why must I accept that no closure is the closure? (From MLA)

You want closure. We do not. Closure means that the provision of fuel will end and do so for good. That is not something that we want. We want your positive fuel through the seduction, your negative fuel through the devaluation and we want to acquire hoover fuel (both positive and negative) thereafter. We want to suck you dry and throw you to one side and then come back for more once you have begun to recuperate and recover. We put effort into seducing you and once you engaged with us then you signed a contract for life which provided that you would always be available for the provision of fuel. It does not matter whether we return in ten days or ten years, we want the ability to return and take fuel from you again. That is why there can be no closure.

It must be on our terms. This accords with our concept of our superiority. You do not have a choice in the matter. If it is your choice, then it amounts to a criticism and this will wound us. This is unacceptable. We do not want you to achieve closure. We always want to keep in place some unfinished business. Whether this is your need to launch a tirade at us because of the way which we have treated you, whether it is because you need answers to so many of the questions that continue to spin around in your head or whether it is because you want to know what we are doing, we need to put in place mechanisms which will always be tempting to you so that you reach out to us. Whether we discarded you or whether you instigated no contact we do not want closure because that means finality. It means the provision of your fuel has ended and we always want fuel. We want your fuel. We want you available for our further machinations because of the contract that you unwittingly signed. We want you available for the triangulation we wish to utilize with our new prospect. We need to keep you on a string, no matter how tenuous so we can jerk it at some point and cause you to jump to our tune once more. If there is closure all the ties are cut. The business becomes finished and you have no reason to want to reach out to you. Thus you become free of us and we can never allow that. This is why some of our most powerful manipulative behaviours such as ever presence is designed to keep the relationship (even if it is just on the basis of memory and thought) alive. Closure is not an option which is acceptable to us.

20. If a narcissist has very, very personal photos of us what does he do with them after the discard/smear? Does he keep them? Or does he normally just delete them when he's done with us? (From Anonymous)

Those personal photos will have been taken either with or without your consent. If the narcissist has not been able to acquire them through his persuasive manner, he will have arranged to have taken them when you did not know they were being taken. There will be a considerable amount of these photos of you in intimate poses and often in humiliating ones too. You will have been told they were just for our use and that if you loved us you would go along with it and many times, caught up in the elation of the golden period you will go along with this. You will be positioned and moved, sometimes in tandem with other people, as we direct and orchestrate you like dolls. This is because this is how we see you. We do not regard you as a person in your own right. We regard you as our appliance and you do as we want.

Even if you will not comply with our wishes we will secure these photos in any event as they will be used during your devaluation and we will threaten to disclose them to the internet at large, to your family, to your workplace and your children's school.

These pictures will not be deleted. They may no longer be on the device but they will have been e-mailed someone secret or downloaded onto a separate hard drive or memory stick for secretion at use at a later stage. We may even show you that these have been deleted in order to lull you into a false sense of security. They may be deleted from the device which we show you, but they will not have been eradicated. These photos are further tools of manipulation which will be used against you post discard. They will be used to smear your name, damage your attempts to instigate a new relationship with someone else and most of all to provoke you into reacting and providing negative fuel. They will be used as bait to hoover you,

"Come back and I will not post those photographs of you at that orgy."

"Just come home and I will promise you that I will delete those pictures I took at that party."

You will be blackmailed by the existence of these photographs to submit to our will and command once again. These photographs will never go. We will always keep them to use against you. You may have to turn to legal remedies to prevent their disclosure and have them delivered up but the simple rule is not to allow them to be taken in the first place. Of course, that is easier said than done when you are dealing with our kind.

21. How do we get back at you when you go no contact?

My kind do not go no contact. That is your device. When you think we have gone no contact what has actually happened is that you are being subjected to a silent treatment. We may have told you that it is over and given you the impression that we have discarded you but what we have done is occupy ourselves with a new primary source, spending time smearing your character with others and preventing you from contacting us. This is a silent treatment. It may last a few days or it could be a few months. This is done in order to make you contact us and plead for a return or even if it is for you to have a tirade at us and call us names, either way it will provide us with negative fuel.

If you want to get back at us when we have subjected you to a silent treatment, the easiest way to do so is to not react. This negates the effect of the silent treatment. If this silent treatment follows your discard you will not hear anything for a period of time because we will be concentrating on the new primary source. Our attempt to cause you to provide negative fuel by subjecting you to a silent treatment has failed and therefore we will leave you alone until such time as we wish to hoover you. If you do not react, this does not provide us with fuel. We need the fuel and we will concentrate on getting it from a different primary source and our supplementary sources. If you want to go further than this cessation of fuel and attack us, you will in effect be instigating a revenge campaign. This is a particular method of attacking our kind and can be launched when we have discarded you and put in place a silent treatment. The revenge campaign requires a particular methodology and mindset and more details on this can be read in the book **Revenge: How to Beat the Narcissist**.

The simplest way however to get back at us during a silent period is to carry on your life as normal, do not contact us, do not do anything which will give us fuel and act as if we do not exist. This will make us seek fuel elsewhere. We will be back for a hoover at some point, but your ignoring us will amount to a criticism and this will cause us injury, meaning we have to get fuel from elsewhere in order to repair the wound which has been caused by your criticism.

22. Do you seek out others besides an empath? (From Debbie)

Yes, we do. The majority of people fall into a category of being normal. These people have empathic traits but not to the same degree and extent as the empath. A normal person would feel concerned if they saw an elderly person trip and fall and that person would stop and help. If a normal person saw a child alone in a shopping centre and in distress that person would intervene to help in some way. Normal people volunteer to help, they donate to charity and generally conduct themselves in a decent manner. Accordingly, these people have empathic traits which are attractive to our kind. They also will have emotional responses to our seduction, our devaluation and the hoovers which will provide us with fuel. These people may make good supplementary sources because they are so voluminous but the output of their fuel is not so potent that they would ever become a primary source. That position is reserved for those who are empaths because of the quality and reliability of their fuel output.

Normal people will be recruited into positions within supplementary sources because they will fulfil a role. They will also be useful for carrying out our campaigns and machinations on our behalf. Indeed, by being less empathic than an empath they are unlikely to question the harm that is being meted out to someone else and they will be more accepting of our behavior along with the charm and brainwashing that accompanies it.

In terms of the provision of fuel, our supplementary sources will be a mixture of high fuel providing empaths and normal people who will still provide fuel but will also provide a valuable role as one of our coterie or as a Lieutenant. They will also be useful for the provision of traits which we acquire to make ourselves appear more attractive.

We also go beyond empaths in terms of those we want to have as primary source and if we already have this position filled with a high fuel giver then we will be delighted to occupy our supplementary sources with additional people who are beyond that of the empath. These are the super empaths and co-dependents. These categories are empaths and then some. These categories of people provide even better fuel, they are much more susceptible to our machinations in terms of fuel provision and control and they are highly prized by our kind. We desire several co-dependents to position about us, one as primary source and others in secondary source positions and if this is not possible we will move down the pecking order seeking super empaths and empaths. The various empathic traits are evident in these individuals and the method by which we target our prospective victims reveals to us the extent and scope of these empathic traits so we can determine that person's category and suitability.

23 Do "lesser Narcissists" actively research techniques online to hone their skills? (From Hope)

This is highly unlikely. The main reason for this is that Lesser Narcissists will not know what they are. They lack the function and awareness to realise what they are and to then understand they have a certain skill set which they could hone and improve. They are unlikely to want to improve it because of two fundamental reasons: -

a. Being a Lesser Narcissist they lack the drive and energy to do so; and
b. They will already have some modus operandi which works for them so they will see no reason to heighten their techniques.

The lesser narcissist sees nothing wrong at all in what he or she does. It is natural to them. The Greater Narcissist knows that the behavior they exhibit is regarded as wrong by society as a whole but they know that it is how they must act to achieve what is to be achieved. They must work in this fashion and if others deem it wrong that is because they have a different outlook. The Greater Narcissist can see that hurt is being caused and would agree, judged by society's standard that this is "wrong" but without any sense of guilt or empathy and the overriding need for the end to justify the means, the Greater Narcissist has no compulsion to alter this behavior.

The Lesser Narcissist by contrast just does as he does. That is the way of things. He lacks insight to understand himself and if anybody should question him about it then that amounts to a criticism and it will ignite his fury. That will end any discussion about his behavior as the Lesser Narcissist engages in the usual tried and trusted methods of physical assault, vicious verbal assaults and damaging property. The techniques of physical and verbal abuse, neither of which will be subtle, the application of intimidation and bullying, allied with threats, means that the Lesser Narcissist has a sufficient arsenal to apply abuse across the arenas of the sexual, physical, emotional and financial. He therefore has no need or awareness to heighten his skill set or alter it by looking up additional information on line. He is what he is and regards there being nothing wrong with what he does. You are the problem and you should shut up and do as you are told.

24. Why do you spoil special occasions? (From Jade)

The short answer is because it is about you and not about us. The spotlight is elsewhere and we not like that. We need the spotlight on us. Special occasions happen every year and you have come to dread the appearance of both your own birthdays and mine. You would much rather neither take place if you are entirely honest. The day is spent treading on eggshells as you await the inevitable argument and dressing down that you will receive. The annual sense of disappointment will happen again and again and you hope somehow it will change, but it never does.

Let's begin with my birthday. You dedicate time and money to making my birthday an enjoyable and memorable occasion. I dedicate a degree of energy to ensure that it is memorable, but for the wrong reasons. You plan something special to mark the occasion and go to considerable lengths to organise a surprise party or a trip out somewhere you believe I will like. You scour catalogues and the Internet trying to find that gift you hope will make me break out in a smile. Most normal people will be happy with half the effort you put into pleasing me on my birthday. Not me. The occasion may involve a grand day out and a spectacular gift but just as it did last year and the year before that, it will end in an argument and us lashing out at you.

On the face of it, one would imagine that just for once we would get throughout the day without causing some kind of drama. After all, the day is all about us. Exactly what we like and what we want. People wish us happy birthday, they send us cards, they give us presents and you run around lifting and carrying for us (even more than usual). The spotlight is firmly on us. We drink up all this fuel but still we want more. Every single second has to be about us. Do not expect us to thank you or anyone else who provides us with a gift. Remember, we are entitled to receive them. We may have received gifts off twenty people but you know that all we will harp on about is the person we did not get a gift from whom we expected to. That becomes the focus of our irritation. The brilliant and thoughtful gifts are left to one side as we rail against this one person who has not bought us something. It does not matter that they sent a card, it does not matter that we did not send them a gift on their birthday (and never have done), and it does not matter that nobody else would expect this distant relative to send such a gift. We will raise it and repeat it and rant about it.

Woe betides you if you do not give to us the exact gift we expected. If you fail to do this, we will comment and lash out at you. You cannot possibly love us since you did not give us the right gift. We conveniently ignore the fact that what you have brought us is still a wonderful gift and we actually do like it. That is not the point. It is not the gift we wanted and you will be subjected to our scathing remarks. If by sheer dint of exhaustive effort, you manage, against all the odds, to work out what we want (don't expect us to help you by explaining what we want, we expect you to know this through telepathy) and give us the right gift, do not expect smiles and thanks. We need to make a scene. Instead, we will remark,

"I see you finally got it right. It does not really make up for all the years you got it wrong does it?"

You can never win when it comes to providing us with gifts. We will always want to put you down no matter what you have done and irrespective of the effort and expense that you have gone to. We will always be unsatisfied and this will manifest in us giving you a dressing down in front of everyone at the party, or storming out of the venue at some sleight. Every year you will hear the same stinging accusation ringing in your ears,

"You've ruined my birthday. Again."

When it comes to your birthday the position is just as bad. We will routinely pretend to forget about it. Do not be fooled by our repeated apparent memory lapses.

We have minds that remember everything and our powers of recall are spectacular. We know your birthday is on the horizon and with most things with us it generates two reactions. On the one hand we resent the forthcoming anniversary because it is a day geared towards the individual, namely you. It is not about us and we cannot stand that. It is rare that you ever allow the spotlight to be shone on you (by now you are so used to having to point it at us, you give up on it ever being fixed on you) but you do hold out the futile notion that it might still be done on your birthday, of all days. We find this galling. This is a day that will be about you and thus where will we get our fuel? Its approach generates dread and horror inside of us.

Conversely, we relish your birthday because we know, despite every previous disappointment, you still hold out hope that this year it might just be different. You pray to your own personal god that please, just for one, the day can pass without incident and you can enjoy yourself. You are not particularly bothered about doing anything special, perhaps a meal out somewhere and the gift need not be expensive, just so long as it exhibits that some kind of thought has gone into it. Your thoughts are based on hope as opposed to expectation. It will not be different because we need to spoil it; we need to make you feel upset and demeaned. To achieve this there are various things that we will do on your birthday.

1.   We forget about it completely. If you mention at 6pm that evening that it is your birthday we will lash out at you by explaining how busy we have been at work or that there has been some other pressing matter which means that it has slipped our minds. We deliberately forget about it and we will not countenance you criticising our omission.

2.   We organise something lavish but we know it is not something you will actually like. As usual, you put a brave face on it and fix a rigid smile to your face. We know what you are really thinking because we know it is not something you like. In fact, it is

more likely that we have organised something that we enjoy. We do this so that everyone else can see what a grand and delightful gesture we have made and we drink in his or her admiration. It also enables us to poke at you repeatedly suggesting that you don't like it. We are goading you into making a tiny admission that it is not quite what you expected and then we erupt in self-indignant fury as we castigate you for being ungrateful after all the effort we have gone to.

3.   We buy some token gesture and point out that your 43rd birthday is not really something to celebrate is it? It is hardly a milestone. We then use this to remark on your advancing years and point out your various flaws.

4.   We organise a lovely birthday for you but spoil it by turning the spotlight back onto ourselves. We turn up late, we flirt with a guest or we manufacture some drama so that everyone is looking at us and not you. We complain at waiters when there is a family meal out, when there is not actual need to do so. We want to make a scene and wrench the spotlight back over to us.

5.   We remember your birthday and spend it doing what you want and we are pleasant to you until early evening when we deliberately pick a fight with you over absolutely nothing. The fuel we gain from this behaviour is all the sweeter as we have built you up, your guarded behaviour has melted away as we appear to have done everything that pleases you. We are waiting. We are waiting for you to feel good and happy and then we will cast you down so your emotional reaction is all the more heightened.

This behaviour is not just reserved for your birthday although we enjoy ruining your birthday the most. We do this with the birthdays of our children, friends and family. We hate it being about someone else and we hate seeing him or her being happy. In our world, nobody else is allowed a birthday and we believe that every day is our birthday and everyone should recognise that and act accordingly.

We know that you would rather your birthday be erased from the calendar. It is always a horrible day in one form or another and you would rather it not take place. We put a big red ring around it in the calendar in our mind and scribble next to the day the words, "Special Fuel Day." The approach that is exhibited above is just as applicable, with appropriate contextual changes to anniversaries, Thanksgiving, Christmas, homecomings, other people's birthdays outside of the family, retirement parties and so on. We use the occasion as a means of getting fuel and this invariably means that it will be spoilt in some way.

25. Do you ever cry? (From Paula)

We use crying, like many of your emotions which we do not experience, as a method of manipulating you. We do not feel guilt, grief or sorrow although we will feel sorry for ourselves. Even though we feel sorry for ourselves we rarely cry because of that feeling since it soon becomes subsumed by our fury that we are made to feel that way and as a consequence of the cruelty of the world and the behaviours of people who are inferior to us. The tears for ourselves are invariably kept at bay as a consequence of our rage at the injustices we suffer. Furthermore, feeling sorry for ourselves will not achieve anything and is a redundant state of affairs which cannot continue for long before we need to find some fuel. We may use feeling sorry for ourselves as a device to the obtain that fuel.

We will cry in order to con you. We can easily turn on the water works for the purpose of drawing concern and sympathy from you. You will usually see our kind cry when we sense that you are on the cusp of leaving us and we have not formulated a new primary source of fuel yet. If we have that primary source and you beat us to the discard, we are not unduly concerned as we will focus on the new primary source and then hoover you at a later stage. If, however we have not yet got that new primary source in place and you tip us off that you are about to go (either by telling us so or we sense you are planning to do it) then we need to keep you in situ. We need to prevent you causing a cessation to our fuel supply (until such time as a new primary source is in place and then we can readily discard you) and one of the ways of doing this is to cry. This usually works for two reasons. The first is that because we do not often cry you are shocked and surprised to see us do so. This immediately gains your attention and suggests that we are treating the situation particularly seriously. The second reason is that because you are an empathic person you will almost always react to the sight of someone being in distress in a positive manner. You will want to help, you will want to ascertain what is wrong and you will also feel guilty if you are the source of this upset and distress. You will want to put it right and listen to our concerns. This display of tears stops you in your tracks and allows us the opportunity to draw fuel from you, gain sympathy and then exert our charm in one of many different ways for the purposes of trying to draw you back in and stop you from leaving us, by means of a Preventative Hoover.

Our tears are always crocodile tears. We do not experience tears of joy. We do not experience true sadness and upset in the way that you do. We cry because it gets us what we want. Just like a child will do.

26. Do you find your existence exhausting? (From Sandy)

It cannot be denied that the ongoing and never-ending question for fuel is one which occupies us on a daily basis. Fuel must be gathered throughout our day. If we receive a good dose of fuel it can power us for several hours without the need for more. Of course, if there is an opportunity to gain some then we will not pass it by. All fuel is welcome but if there is a good provision of fuel early on this will allow me to get on with other things and not be concerned about the provision of fuel. Accordingly, in such a situation this is not exhausting at all. It may be that I receive an injection of fuel first thing which powers me into early afternoon. I obtain a similar dollop of fuel which can take me into late afternoon and then more which takes me through into the evening with another dose that sees me through until I retire to bed.

In between those times I may gather more fuel purely as a consequence of my interactions. Fuel is always the focus and I will not turn it away. It may be that owing to what I do during that day or how it pans out that I do not receive any fuel in between but that does not concern me as the injections of fuel at the times described are sufficiently strong and of good volume to sustain me. On other occasions I may find myself gathering fuel all day from different sources and in different amounts, just getting enough to power me until the next injection. That will involve lots of interactions and machinations but I do not find them exhausting because each time I receive the fuel, it makes me feel stronger and powerful and therefore the effort expended in obtaining it is replenished and worthwhile.

What is exhausting is if I do not receive the fuel and I begin to grow restless and weak. Then the hunt for fuel, in this weakened state does take its toll and I find it exhausting. Fortunately, owing to the way I operate and all of the sources that I have put in place this rarely happens.

27. Are you every sorry for what you do? Do you ever express regret for your actions and all the horrible things that you have done? If not, why not? (From Serena)

We do not engage in showing remorse. We know how to say sorry. We should do because we hear you say it often enough. We never feel sorry for anything that we do. Why should we? We never do anything wrong. Everything is always somebody else's fault, usually yours. In line with our sense of entitlement we are allowed to do as we please. Since that is the case, how can anything ever be our fault? When you demand that we apologise you offend us considerably. This is for several reasons.

1. Who are you to expect us to apologise? You are inferior to us and you do what we want. It is not the other way around.

2. An apology is an admission of wrongdoing. In case you somehow missed it, we do not do anything wrong.

3. Remorse is exhibiting weakness. We are not weak. You are.

4. You are being assertive. We do not like that as it threatens our control over you. We must have compliance. If we do not, we run the risk of losing fuel.

5. If you expect us to apologise in front of others you will have a long wait. We must never lose face. What you can expect from us is a savage reaction behind closed doors for you having the audacity to try to embarrass us in this way.

We are genuinely baffled when you suggest to us that we ought to be sorry for something that has happened. It just does not compute with us. The reason for this is that to show remorse we understand that one has to understand how the other person has been hurt or affected in some way. We have no time available to be thinking about how others may be affected by what we do. Even if we did, we lack the capacity to understand the feelings of others, as we have not been designed in such a way. This empathic approach has been denied to us. We give thanks that that is the case because we see exactly what happens to such people. They get dragged into a life of servitude to our need to acquire fuel. We shudder to think that that could actually happen to us.

Remorse is an important state to you. As an empathic individual you have no difficulty in apologising and expressing your regret for something that has happened or for something that you may have done (or failed to have done). You regard this as an integral part of being a well-adjusted individual. We know this because we have heard you speak about this on many occasions. We know that you understand the concept of remorse because you are able to place yourself in the other person's shoes. If you ever respond to somebody in a short-tempered fashion and they protest, you either know what it feels like (because you have experienced it yourself - something which has certainly happened when you have been entangled with our kind) or you are capable of working out how it must feel because of your naturally ability to express empathy. As a consequence of this, you expect us to be able to express remorse also. You expect this attribute of other people and it confuses you to find that we are incapable of doing so. You will fall into the trap of trying to demonstrate what we have done wrong in order to then reach a state of remorse. All you are doing is giving yourself a mountain to climb and then when you think you have reached the peak; another mountain is revealed beyond the first. Oh and we are pulling on your rope trying to wrench you from the mountainside as you try to climb.

Not only are we incapable of feeling remorse and that we maintain adamantly that we have nothing to apologise for because we do nothing wrong, there is a further reason for our failure to ever express remorse. The majority of the time you want us to apologise and show sorrow for the horrible things that we have done to other people and mainly you. In our minds you are asking us to apologise for breathing.

Why is that? You need to breathe to survive. We do as well but we also need to behave in this unpleasant way to survive. Our nasty treatment of you, the silences, the manipulation and the intimidation are all our methods of keeping you under control and providing us with fuel. We have to do it. Accordingly, by expecting us to show remorse for these behaviours you are expecting us to apologise for a fundamental and necessary action that in our world is akin to the need to eat, breathe, drink and sleep.

You would never contemplate saying sorry for having spent eight hours asleep would you? That is why we do not consider there is any need for us to apologise for this basic requirement to securing our existence. You point out however that your need for sleep does not harm someone else. You must sleep otherwise your will become fatigued, exhausted and ultimately ill. Going to sleep is not an act, which causes a consequence to somebody else whereas our bullying behaviour affects others. Your analysis appears correct except that we do not recognise you as someone else, someone separate and distinct from us. You are an extension and the harm that you may suffer from our necessary behaviour is just part of the equation. It is a by-product of a process, like exhaust fumes from an engine. Those fumes pollute and poison, much in the way that our behaviour is described but the engine must still run in the same way that our behaviours must take place if we are to survive. The necessity of this and our failure to regard you as a separate entity means that we cannot see any valid reason (even if we were capable of expressing it) for being remorseful about our conduct.

The only occasion when you will find us expressing some kind of remorse is when it suits our purposes. You must be aware that this expression is false. It is yet again a learned behaviour. We even hate to pretend to be remorseful because it smacks so much of weakness and that is something that we abhor. We will use it however when we sense that it is needed to avoid something worse from happening to us. This is usually the threat that we are about to lose a supply of fuel. If we recognise that you are going to leave us, we will put on our most contrite of appearances (whilst stifling our sniggers) and issue a mealy-mouthed apology for our behaviour. We will not actually be considering what that behaviour is because we are too focused on ensuring that this ruse works and we prevent you from leaving us. We do not give any consideration to the supposed error of our ways. We do not listen to the lecture that you are giving us, your emphasis on changing and improving or whatever other sanctimonious drivel you are spouting, we just want you to accept our apology and remain as a source of fuel. Notice how we never appear sorry or apologetic when we do not stand to lose something. Pay attention to how suddenly we can deploy our expression of contrition. Only yesterday we had been subjecting you to silent treatment and displaying our customary haughtiness towards you. Today you pack a suitcase and appear to be leaving us so we immediately realise we are in the Last Chance Saloon and decide that a display of false remorse is what is required. Our ability to switch from such unpleasant treatment to issuing a supposed apology is a clear indicator of the falsity of our sorrow. If we truly meant that we are sorry, we would not have been behaving in the way we did in the first place.

Keep in mind the number of times that we have supposedly expressed remorse and then repeated the behaviour. Do you find yourself thinking that you have experienced this before? Do you say to yourself that you have heard our apologies previously and you are going to leave and this time you mean it? Those are clear signs to you that we are leading you on a merry dance with this further form of manipulation. We know that deep down you do not want to go. We have deployed a variety of means to keep you hooked and we know that all you want is to hear us apologise. You truly believe that deep down inside of us there is some good and by saying sorry we are letting this rise to the surface. You are a good person and your worldview is that other people must be good as well, even those who appear to act to the contrary most of the time. Your view is entirely understandable given the type of person that you are but you are wasting your time if you ever expect a heartfelt and meaningful expression of remorse from us.

You will however fall for our empty apology. Once we see you nod and accept what we have said we feel the relief and then a surge of power. Our manipulation of you has worked again. There is every chance that what we have just falsely apologised for, we will go and do again within 24 hours. That is our way of maintaining power and also our method of sticking two fingers up at you.

Do not expect sorrow or remorse from us. It will not happen.

28. Why do you not tell us what you are thinking about when we ask? Why will you not share your thoughts with us? What are you thinking about? (From Rebecca)

It is both a blessing and a curse for you to have to know what people are thinking and feeling. The uncharitable might label you as nosey. You do it because you like to be able to know this to enable you to respond in the most constructive and pleasant fashion. If someone is having a difficult day and is plagued with unpleasant thoughts, you want to know about it. You can then offer words of encouragement and support. Should someone be in a good mood you are pleased for him or her and want to be able to share in that positive experience.

When your kind become ensnared by us you have no or little understanding of what is happening. You need to seek out answers in order to fathom out why we are behaving as we are. Our actions and words lack logic and this flies contrary to the way you operate. Not only do you need to understand why we are doing what we are doing, you also want to be able to help.

"How can I help you if you do not tell me what it is that is wrong?"

"If you do not talk to me, I cannot help you and I want to help you."

"Why won't you tell me what the problem is? If you do, I am sure we can work it out."

"Keeping it to yourself is not going to help. A problem shared and all that."

Do you recognise those comments and questions?

We won't tell you what we are thinking. First of all, we want you to guess. We love to play games and having you try to work out what is going on in our minds is a game we do like to indulge in. Keeping you guessing means you keep paying us attention and that means fuel. Secondly, this will ensure you remain in a state of confusion. We do not want you to work out why we behave as we do and we do not want you to know what is going on in our heads. You remain confused and bewildered and that means we are able to exert our control over you for longer. By keeping you confused, we heighten your anxiety, which in turn will tire you out. This will result in your coping mechanisms becoming depleted and as a consequence you will become more malleable to our manipulative conduct.

Thirdly, we are of the firm opinion that you should already know what we are thinking. Yes, I realise this is contradictory to our desire to have you know what is going in our minds, but we are a myriad of contradictions because we are entitled to be this way. You should know what we want before we even want it. You should be anticipating our needs and requirements. If you fail to do so, then you must not love us. That is the conclusion that we reach. We think that you cannot be bothered to consider our needs and we regard your behaviour as being contrary to our wellbeing. It is of no consequence to us that you do not have telepathic powers, that we do not tell you what we are thinking about or what we want, you are expected to know. This is because as an innately superior person our needs should be anticipated and met. Since you are beneath us, this is the role to which you have been assigned and you should deliver. Do not bleat to us about the impossibility of your task and how we do not help you fathom out what we want, we have much more important matters to attend to. You are becoming a distraction and you risk incurring our wrath.

Fourthly, we love to be regarded as enigmatic. By creating this appearance of depth we feel powerful and god-like. Our kind is shallow and base creatures and depth is something beyond our grasp although we covet it. In order to fabricate that sense of depth we attempt to create an air of mystery about us. Do not disturb us as we sit staring out of the window looking across the view. We want you thinking that we are embroiled in deep and philosophical considerations. We can see you from the corner of your eye looking on in admiration.

"He seems so lost in thought, it must be something important."

"I wonder what mammoth principles he is grappling with right now?"

"If only I could equal what is going on in the great mind right now."

This is what we tell ourselves that you are thinking as you look at us. Yes, we are great, yes we are masters of deep contemplation and such is the weight of our thoughts that you will not be able to carry them. Do not even try to do that. Do not ask what we are thinking about, you cannot possibly understand. We do not want you to shatter the illusion that we are creating that we are people of substance and engaged in wrestling with thoughts beyond your comprehension.

Finally, and ultimately, we do not want you to ask us what we are thinking because we do not want to tell you what is actually running through our minds. We do not want to divulge the dark thoughts that course through our consciousness. That would give the game away. We do not want you to realise that our thoughts actually operate on a fairly limited level. Yes, we are articulate, knowledgeable and well-read but all we do then is regurgitate what we have learned. I have told you about our formidable powers of recall. We are experts at copying and absorbing as we take on the personas and personalities as others. We hijack ideas and pass them off as our own, we can repeat that wonderful part of Hamlet's soliloquy and we will sing all the verses of a particularly beautiful song but we are but a magpie. We dart in and steal from others and pretend that the pilfered item is ours.

The only real creative thoughts that we engage in are associated with one thing; the acquisition of fuel. Where can we get it from next? How will we do it? What will the best way to achieve it? Who can we secure it from and how much? What methods should we engage to bring about the flow of delicious, sweet, sweet fuel?

What are we thinking? We are devising, planning and plotting. We are constructing lies and fallacies to obtain our fuel. We are building more of our fictitious world and generating more of our fantasy. Our Machiavellian minds are engrossed in the dark and the nefarious. These considerations revolve around seducing you and others, our schemes envelope the savage devaluing of you, casting you down from the pedestal and subjecting you to our dark arts. Do not ask what we are thinking. We won't say for the reasons outlined above and in truth, do you really want to know what is going on inside our evil minds?

29. Do you believe that you will remain in control of fuel forever? (From Susan)

There appear to be two answers to this question. Firstly, do I believe that when I engage with a new source of fuel, do I believe that I will remain in control of that source forever? Secondly, do I believe that I will remain in control of my fuel supply (no matter where it comes from) forever? I shall address both questions.

Dealing with the first question, yes I believe that I will be in control of that source forever because the power of my manipulation is extensive and I have seen it work on so many occasions before. I have explained above that when you engage with us you sign an unwritten contract that you will always provide us with fuel and it is on this contract that we base our control of you. We seduce you and receive the positive fuel from you. You provide this willingly and who would not want to be subjected to the golden period? Gaining control of your fuel in this manner is fairly easy. We gain negative fuel during your devaluation. Provoking you to provide us with this fuel is straightforward because of what has gone before and the methods of manipulation that we utilize against you. Thereafter if we discard you, it is only temporary because we reserve the right to come back and gather fuel from you again at some unspecified point in the future and on unspecified occasions. If you try and escape us, we will come after you for fuel through the Grand Hoover. If that succeeds we have regained control of you as a fuel source again. If it does not work, well you still belong to us in our minds as a fuel source and we will apply follow-up hoovers thereafter. We may not be actually obtaining fuel from you but we retain the right to do so and therefore in our minds this equates to retaining control over you as a fuel source. Our right to extract fuel from you exists in perpetuity.

Turning to the second question. The answer is another yes. I must have fuel. I need it to exist and therefore I will ensure that I shall have the means to obtain fuel and the supply lines in place to receive it. The sources and methods of supply may alter over time according to my energy levels and the environments that I am in but my need for fuel is such that I will also hold control over how I gain my fuel.

I may, as I become old, not get out as much, but I will still draw fuel from family who visit, one or two friends I may have retained, my visiting nurse, the doctor and through the use of telephone and technology. Put me in prison and I will draw fuel from the inmates, prison guards, visitors, pen pals, the smuggled mobile phone which will be utilized for the pursuit of fuel and my frequent interactions with the prison psychologist. Put me on a rocky and deserted island and I will do my upmost to bring a ship to me, like some modern day siren, to gather fuel and then escape my confinement. I will always find a way to obtain fuel. Where's there is a will and there is always a will, there's a way, there is always a way to get my fuel.

30. If I flirt with somebody else in front of you, how does it make you feel? Is this a good way of getting back at you or not? (From Melissa)

We are allowed to flirt. You are not. Such a contradiction should come as no surprise to you by now. We use flirtation to draw our victims into our web and thereafter as a mild form of triangulation to provoke an emotional reaction from those we are meant to be committed to. It is entirely permissible for us to be flirtatious, although I do not actually regard it as such conduct. I see it as being friendly, taking an interest in people and fulfilling my role as someone that people are naturally drawn to. As I have had to tell jealous partners in the past, I cannot help being popular and if you want to remain with me, you will need to get used to it. Naturally, I know what I am doing with the choice words, carefully gauged tactile gestures and suggestive comments. I am gathering fuel from the individual who is now caught in the glare of my sizzling laser beams, pinned to the spot by my flattering comments and witty badinage. All the while we can sense you glowering nearby, not daring to say anything or do anything to interrupt our display and more importantly our feeding on this fuel, but sufficiently irritated to provide us with another fuel line.

I have seen some of you decide that the best way to deal with us is to use our own behaviour against us. Admittedly, that can work with some of our manipulative ways. It usually results in us shutting off that particular technique and opening up a different front. Do not make the mistake of flirting in front of us however. You are giving us the green light to go on the attack. Should you do this, you have cut off a supply of fuel to us. You are not reacting to our treatment of you, as we desire, by you becoming jealous and silently raging in a corner. Instead you are being assertive and you are challenging our superiority. This is not permitted. Furthermore, you are making us look foolish in front of other people. Worst of all, you are telling the recipient of your flirtation that you are a free agent. You are not. You belong to us. You are our property. You are our appliance. You do not work for anyone other than us. You are telling us that we are not good enough and that you have found somebody better than us. We cannot comprehend that being the case. Nobody is better than us. Have you forgotten all the wonderful things that we did for you when we were seducing you? Have you cast to one side all the magnificent gestures and words that we used? How dare you throw all of that back in our faces? You are selfish, slutty and you disgust us.

This attack against us is on several fronts.

1.	The removal of fuel;

2.	The challenge to our superiority

3.	You are diminishing our standing.

None of this can be deemed as acceptable. You should have grasped that we regularly adopt double standards. What we do is fine but you must not do it and we will stand and berate you about your conduct having behaved exactly the same way only moments earlier and not bat an eyelid at our outrageous hypocrisy. We do not like it when people use our tools against us. We fashioned those tools, you did not.

If you are fortunate, we will log your transgression and then subject you to retribution once we are home. It is likely we will take steps to record your behaviour. You may notice this but emboldened by your assertive behaviour and also we can see you are enjoying the reaction you are getting from us (who is displaying the narcissistic tendencies now eh?) you continue with the behaviour and increase it. We will make a note of what you are doing in accurate detail in our minds and ally it with some footage. Notwithstanding the times you have replayed our own conduct back to us, which we have denied and avoided, we will do the same to you. We will also make a great show of exhibiting it to other people to underline what a horrible person you are and your treatment of us is despicable. We will then exact our revenge against you behind closed doors and let you know just how mightily you have offended us.

In certain instances, the indignant fury that you unleash in us by flirting with somebody offends us to such a degree that we lose control there and then. We fly into a rage and haul you away from the object of your affections. Should they try and intervene they will also be subjected to our anger and more than likely physically. We will dress you down in front of everyone else and it is highly likely we will force you to leave early, our nasty insults echoing behind as we leave the venue. By this point we care little for what people might think about our outburst, we are comforted by the fact that we know it is your fault. Should anyone raise our explosion with us we will explain how it was your fault that we ended up doing this, that anybody else would have done the same in such a situation and invite them to speak to you, as you are the real villain of the piece, not us.

Your attempts to deflect blame back onto us will not work. Even though we routinely flirt with people that of course if our birthright. We are masters at it and it is a tool of our trade. You are not permitted to copy us. You must know your place. Trying to use one of our methods against us is not wise move and will have very definitely unpleasant consequences for you.

31. Is every "move" that you make, every word that you speak, calculated, always about an agenda? (From RW)

Everything that we say and do is calculated to provide us with fuel. Much of it is instinctive. Those of our kind who are lesser in nature will behave a certain way because he or she is programmed to do that without thinking and they will not regard what they do as conforming to some agenda it is "just what they do". Should you challenge them that they are advancing some agenda you will be met with a denial. This is because the lesser of our kind do not operate to an agenda they have any awareness about. They react and function as a matter of need. They will do things without necessarily realizing the reason they are doing it, just that that is the way things are. The lesser narcissist will do some planning. He will plan his seduction of somebody by identifying the target but again much of it will be based on instinct and reaction. He will know that he feels restless and needs fuel (although he will not think of it as fuel) and knows that he needs to gain attention from somebody and he will consider how to do it. The Lesser Narcissist operates with a small amount of planning. Much of what he does will be based on instinct and reaction. He will conform to an agenda although he will not realise it.

By contrast, the Greater Narcissist is a master planner. We regard people as pieces on a chess board that we move around as we put in place our machinations. We consider who will make the best targets and plan our seduction of those people. We too respond by instinct as well but there is far more planning and calculation taking place with the Greater Narcissist. We consider the import of what we say, we ruminate on whether someone is being disloyal and how we might deal with them, we consider the best way to obtain fuel or to manipulate somebody. We consider whether there are any threats and how they should be dealt with. We of the Greater variety are systematic and methodical. We know what we want and we plan how to get it. We are great schemers as we plot our triangulations and wheels within wheels. There is always some scheme or plan being hatched. You should be most wary of the narcissist who is sat quiet with a pensive look on his or face because we are most likely scheming the next move against you and other people.

32. Do you honestly feel superior to me & everyone else? (From Denise)

Yes. We are innately superior to you and other people by virtue of who we are. Our sense of superiority forms one of the narcissistic pillars (see **Revenge: How to Beat the Narcissist** for more details) and therefore is central to the concept of what we are. Our sense of superiority is based on perception and also necessity.

We see ourselves as superior because of the traits which we possess and those that we acquire from other successful and superior people. By acquiring those traits, we regard them as part of us and this only goes to underline our superiority. We are better than you at many things. We are better athletes, better looking, possess better bodies, better minds, we are leaders in our fields, we are better artists, musicians, dancers, hosts, comedians, businessmen, doctors, lawyers, architects, engineers and so on. The traits of success mean that we must be superior otherwise why are we successful?

The necessity of being superior provides us with the drive and the motivation to maintain control over you. If we regarded you as an equal, we would be far more relaxed about the things that you do and this would lessen our control over you and thus the supply of fuel would be adversely affected. If we regarded you as an equal, we would allow you to come and go as you please. This means you would have a more active social life without us. This means that you would be influenced by other people and more likely to break away from us, but also it means that you would not be with us as often to provide us with fuel. You would also have a break from our malign influences which diminished the effectiveness of our manipulation. BY considering you inferior, we adopt an almost paternalistic approach by deciding what you should do, where you should go, who you should see and so on. This allows us to maintain control over you. We know best for you because we are of an elevated status. You do not understand but we do. We are doing it for your own good. This superiority is the driver behind how we control you. It also means that if you do not adhere to our demands and control, then your impertinence at challenging out superiority results in our fury igniting with the consequences thereafter which enable us to exert control over you once again and re-establish the natural order of things with us at the helm and you below decks chained to the oars.

Our superiority is based on the perception we have of ourselves. This is based on our actual successes and those we purloin from others. This superiority is also essential to ensure we control you and therefore gain the fuel which is necessary to preserve out existence.

33. Why do you make it so damn to work you out? Why am I always left trying to second guess your intentions? Why can't you just take my fuel and be straightforward? (From Kathryn)

We want and demand that you spend your time trying to second-guess what we will say and do. This makes us feel powerful and omniscient and at the same time it will exhaust you and leave you unable to cope. This lessens the risk that you will find the strength to try to leave us and remove that supply which we hold so dear.

Through the application of our manipulative techniques we push you into a position where you are left having to ascertain what we might do in order to please us and most of all to try to escape our wrath. This is a near constant state of vigilance where you are treading on eggshells as you try to negotiate your way through another day. It is hard. It is unpredictable. It is designed to condition you to our way of thinking so that you keep on supplying us. It is a method of control and it is utterly damaging to you.

We enjoy you trying to second-guess what we do so much because it makes us feel like a god. Before you do anything you must consider whether it will please or annoy us. It also strips you of your identity. You no longer think for yourself but you have to change your thinking to consider what we want. I wrote above how you can never make us see the world in the way that you do. Not only will we not change so that can be achieved, we will alter the way you look at the world. We force you to regard the world through our eyes. Your decisions are no longer your own as everything must be considered against our matrix. You become our attachment, your self-esteem melts away and you become our appliance. We regard getting you to this position as the pinnacle of achievement. You have become an automaton that is geared to establishing what our needs are and fulfilling them. Should you not do so then you will suffer the consequences by being subjected to one of our vicious rages.

The problem you face is that we cannot be completely second-guessed because we keep changing the rules and the circumstances. I have written elsewhere how some people regard being ensnared by a narcissist as being trapped in some kind of prison. It is worse than that. In prison there are rules and conventions which if obeyed means that your period of incarceration will pass quicker and without incident. Stand in that place, be quiet at this time, and do not look at him. Rules both formal and informal to be adhered to so that you do not feel the wrath of prisoner or prisoner guard. There are no such rules when we trap you. It is akin to being in a concentration camp where as the camp commandant we can do as we please, whenever we please and in whatever manner suits us and you have no way of knowing whether the next thing that you will do will lead to you being shot. The way we change our minds and our behaviours, so that last week we liked a particular food but now we do not want to eat it makes your life extremely difficult. Not only is this random nature difficult to address, when you fail to do as required (and you will) you are punished with blistering fury at your failure to appreciate us and give us what we want. You are expected to know at all times what we will want and need, even if it changes at a moment's notice.

Someone who is subjected to his for long periods will be made ill. The hyper vigilance combined with the erratic behaviour and repeated chastisement will take its toll on you. Trying to second-guess us is exhausting and ultimately futile. Yes, we want it but the cost to you of doing this will be substantial. You lose your identity and your sense of self. You are exhausted and anxious from being a state of high alertness nearly all the time. You feel unsettled and jumpy. You forget who you are and the concept of relaxation has become alien to you. You are treated horrendously being insulted and shouted at when all you have tried to do is the right thing. Subjected to this for any length of time will result in a major breakdown for you.

Do not fall into the trap of trying to second-guess us. You may like to please, it is in your nature, but this is trying to please someone who can never be pleased. You are condemning yourself to a form of slavery and ultimately illness.

34. Is flattery the one thing that I can use to control and manipulate you? (From E)

You are not able to control all of our kind. You are only ever able to prevent our control over you by the application of certain techniques and measures which are described in greater detail in **Escape, No Contact** and **Revenge.** You can use flattery to provide positive fuel but you will have to make it appear genuine otherwise we will notice the insincerity and we will regard this as a criticism of us. Our fury will then be ignited and we will lash out at you. Flattery will serve you best with a Lesser or Mid-Range Narcissist whose level of functioning may not see through the falsity of your flattery and instead be grateful to accept the compliments and lavish praise that you are providing. With the Greater of our kind, any lack of sincerity will be detected.

Flattery will serve some purpose against the Lesser and Mid-Range Narcissists by enabling you to bring about a desired response from them. For example, if you want to go to a particular restaurant but do not wish to say that you want to go there because you anticipate we will regard that as you asserting yourself rather than submitting to our naturally superior decision-making, you may say something along the lines of: -

"I wondered whether you would like to go to Sabatini's because they cooked a really good steak for you and the waiting staff enjoyed your stories? Shall we go again?"

By making it about you and how you shone there your flattery will be more likely to bring about the desired response that we go to this restaurant.

Flattery can also be used to disarm us. You may find yourself under attack and by seeking to escape the worst of the attack you can admit your wrong-doing and thank us for pointing out that we had gone wrong. The criticism you may have made earlier which ignited our fury has been removed and therefore the need for the continuing ignited fury will be diminished and ultimately extinguished.

Flattery can be used to your advantage but it must be exercised with caution as if your narcissist detects that you are manipulating him or her (and after all as master manipulators we are attuned to this) there will be an ignition of fury with the usual consequences.

35.. It seems narcissists don't have a lot of respect for their 'victims'; is that always the case? Do they sometimes target someone they do respect purely with the intention of bringing them down? (From Megan)

The word victim is a broad church. In the widest sense it can be applied to anybody who interacts with our kind. Even the barista in our coffee shop who we are always pleasant to and who gives us extra re-fills without us asking is a victim even though they may not regard themselves as having suffered in some way. In the same way that you can be convicted of drug dealing even if you give it away rather than take money, the concept of a victim of a narcissist extends to those who have interacted with the narcissist even if they do not feel like they have suffered. The reality is that anyone who has interacted with our kind has been conned in some way. They may not have suffered as an outcome, but they have been duped and conned by our false personae. Accordingly, anyone who is a primary, secondary or tertiary source is a victim of the narcissist. This will include people who we do not harm but ensnare for the purposes of drawing fuel from the positive reactions but especially for the purpose of acquiring some of that person's traits for ourselves. The concept of us respecting somebody is not quite true. The best that might be said is that we have an admiration for somebody based on their usefulness to us in providing traits that we can acquire. Successful people fall into this category. We are unlikely to devalue them as we want them to like us, allow us to socialise with them and accordingly benefit through our association with them which enables us access to their traits. These people are probably the nearest concept of respect that you will find with our kind and it would serve no purpose to us if we were to try and do them down. Accordingly, you will not find us targeting someone like this, that we almost respect, in order bring them down. It is correct to say however that we do not have any respect for all of our other victims, including those who would be regarded as the victim in the truest sense, because they have suffered at our hands. If we respected these people we would not do what we do to them. We would not con them, hoax them, dupe them and then abuse them. We have no respect for our victims that we draw fuel from as we do not regard them as people with their own identities. We consider them to be appliances which are there to serve a purpose for us and provide us with what we need.

36 Why can't I get you out of my head? (From Denise)

There are two fundamental reasons for this. The first is the concept of ever presence and the second is because we create unfinished business. Ever presence is a pleasing consequence of all the hard work I invested in the Love Bombing technique. In order to overload your senses and sweep you up in my enticing whirlwind of love and affection I did numerous things to ensnare you.

I took you to a park and kissed you beneath a spreading oak tree, pushing you gently against the trunk as I whispered in your ear that this was our tree and we would always come back here and kiss beneath its huge boughs. I ensured that several songs became indelibly imprinted in your mind to remind you of you and me being together. I just didn't go for the romantic ones though. No, I ensured that I selected a range of music to accompany every mood and emotion. That upbeat dance track that is associated with our marvellous holiday in Ibiza. That slow waltzing song that we held each other to and listened to on the balcony of my apartment. That frenetic and energetic rock track that we both jumped around to in your living room. You marveled at how I managed to select certain songs and pieces of music that you loved and seemed so apt for the moment we were caught up in. You did not know that I had already spent time studying the YouTube videos of songs you adore on your Facebook news feed. I have also wheeled out this playlist to several other victims and I know it works.

I made sure that you would repeatedly see me sat in the same seat in your kitchen reading a Terry Pratchett book. You would then make dinner as I read aloud to you. We always had a bottle of Rioja on a Wednesday evening. I selected four particular restaurants and took you to them repeatedly. I engaged my lieutenants in reinforcing all the wonderful memories associated with dinner parties, trips to the coast and sporting events. Every day there would be a poem left for you under your pillow. I devoured box sets of Breaking Bad, Poldark and West Wing with you. I even learned pieces of the dialogue, which I would repeat from time to time.

I specifically wore the same fragrance, used the same anti-perspirant and shower gel so that this created a particular cocktail of scents, which are forever linked to me. My washing powder and fabric conditioner were chosen to stand out for you. Little do you know I have a notebook, which lists each ex-girlfriend and a corresponding list of smells that I used when I was with you. For you it was Chanel Allure Sport, Dove Men and Care Clean deodorant and Molton Brown Black Peppercorn Body Wash. Not that you have forgotten that have you?

The dedication by which I ensured I had imprinted myself on your life in every conceivable sense was worthwhile. Not only did I draw you in and ensnare you, but I also left my mark on you so that once I had discarded you (or if you made the bold move of leaving me) I would forever remain with you.

You walk through the park and you are haunted by the image of us up against the oak tree. Somebody gets in the lift next to you wearing Chanel Allure and you want to reach out and hug him as you are immediately taken back to smelling me lying next to you in bed. When *With or Without You* is played you start to sob as you recall how I held you close during a thunderstorm as it played in the background (on repeat of course). Everything I did during the Love Bombing was calculated to trap you but was also laying the ground for infecting the afterwards with me. You see me in books, taste me in certain foods and hear my voice when watching a re-run of a programme. You try to escape by avoiding certain things that are poignant reminders, but that means cutting out certain things that you enjoy. Should you make that sacrifice to someone like me? You are torn. Even if you exercise such discipline, I have planted enough reminders around you that you cannot and will not escape me.

You go to the newsagents and see The Times newspaper and instantly remember show I would read it on a Sunday as we lounged after making love through the morning. The powerful memory hurts. I am a spectre that follows you everywhere you go. I know this is happening and it gives me a wonderful sense of omnipotent power. I know that I am in your head and heart on a daily basis. I know how much pain this will be causing you. I also know that I still have several hooks deep inside you and it will not take much if I decided to throw a line to you to draw you back in.

- Such an attention to detail has reaped several rewards.
- I drew you in.
- I remain with you through my ever presence.
- I cause you pain.
- I feel omnipotent.
- I have the means to draw you in again, like a sleeper cell planted inside you.

It is stunningly effective and in the phase of ever presence I do not actually have to do anything because the hard work was done many months ago during my Love bombing of you. You keep triggering it through the things you do and the memories which you have.

In terms of unfinished business, we create a situation where there is no closure for you. You have questions you want to ask us, situations you still need to understand and a huge desire to be able to say your piece to us. To achieve this, we create a situation where you have a need to contact us. You want to ask us why we treated you this way, you want to know whether we did really love you or not, we want to know if you are happy with the new person we have on our arm and what have they got that we have not? You want the opportunity to launch into a tirade and give us a piece of your mind. There are unanswered questions and unfinished business and this makes it so hard for you to resist. You know that you should not engage with us but you want to find out why we did as we did because we just vanished and left you wondering and pondering. You want to understand why we treated you so badly when all you ever did was love us, because, in your world, that makes no sense. These two elements; the ever presence and the unfinished business results in the temptation to reach out to us being very difficult to resist.

You cannot get us out of your head because on the one hand you do not want to because you do not want us to be lost to you. No matter how badly you have been treated you still hope beyond hopes that we will return and everything will be alright again. You keep dredging up the old memories from the golden period and in doing so you are keeping us in your head. Add to this the effects of ever presence which we purposefully put in place as we love bombed you and then the creation of unfinished business and you will find that you have a situation where we have taken occupation in your head, even though we are no longer physically around and it is so very difficult to evict us.

37. What red flags exist in the beginning from all four types of narcissist? (From Tammy)

There are many red flags which fly at the outset of your engagement with our kind and abusers in general, many of which bear some similarity. For considerable detail on those red flags I recommend to you **Red Flag: 50 Warning Signs of Narcissistic Seduction,** which will prove an eye-opener. Not all of these flags apply to the four cadres of narcissist (Victim, Somatic, Cerebral and Elite) but some do. I think that one which stands out is the desire of all four cadres of narcissist to bind the victim to them as quickly as possible. Each type of narcissist acts with unreasonable haste in order to tie the victim to him or her for the purposes of ensuring that there is a steady and reliable source of potent fuel. Accordingly, if someone you are interacting with makes a declaration of love very soon, wants to co-habit, get engaged or married and/or wants to have a child with you, that is a particular red flag which is applicable to all four cadres. I expand on this theme of why we do this in a further answer in this book.

Another red flag which is applicable to all four cadres of narcissist is the act of mirroring. This is a technique whereby we like the things which you like and dislike those things which you do not enjoy. This results in the creation of a connection between us and our victims and causes the victim to feel closer to us. This is an evident red flag which occurs with all types of narcissist.

A further red flag in common is the use of incessant messaging for the purposes of the seduction. This technique which makes the victim feel that him or her is at the centre of the narcissist's attention and universe and thus causes them to increase their own affections for the narcissist as part of the love-bombing which takes place, is common to all four types. Even the lowly Victim Narcissist will make use of this technique as it is effective and easy to implement from his position lying on the sofa in front of the television.

Another common red flag is that all of these narcissists will be scathing about their exes as part of their ongoing devaluation of that person and in order to make the new prospect feel sorry for the narcissist that they have endured a troubled time with someone else. By slating your predecessor, you are made out to be even more special since you are nothing like that horrible person. It is also designed to make you feel more secure, since we do not want anything to do with your predecessor so you need not be worried about us still having feelings for an ex. Of course this situation will change when we want to partake of the hoover fuel that we will receive from this person, but during the seduction you will be repeatedly told how horrible this person was and is.

These are some of the prominent red flags which are applicable to all four of the categories of narcissists and you can read more about them in the publication mentioned above.

38. I work with at least two of your kind, what I would like to know is why you never let anybody else claim the credit for things and why you must always take it for yourself? Surely you can allow other people to share in the plaudits? (From Mags)

This section is primarily concerned with business and work. As I have explained above, we are creatures of economy and prefer for other people to do the legwork. This also means that we like other people to come up with the brilliant, new idea and thus we are then in a position to take the credit for that idea ourselves. We are magpies. If something shiny and sparkling is put in front of us, we will happily snatch it and claim that it belongs to us.

If you find that you are working with one of my kind, any kind of novel proposal, good idea or money-saving scheme that you may think of will be appropriated by me. You work for me and therefore I regard it as your obligation to do things, which make me look good. Moreover, if it were not for the marvellous way that I have trained you, you would not have the skill set or ability to think of this point. In reality, I created it and allowed you to nurture it before returning it to me. You are not really equipped to have the big ideas, I have furnished you with the ability to generate something, which needs to be relayed to me so that I can finesse it and then present it as mine. I gain the credit and you gain the reward of not being subjected to one of my withering tirades against your competence and commitment.

My kind is especially apt at doing this with their children. We do not praise them for their accomplishments but instead gain power by claiming their achievement is down to us. It gives us fuel in a vicarious fashion. Our child has performed excellently in examinations and rather than congratulating him or her on their performance, we proclaim that their cerebral excellence is all down to us.

"He gets his brains from me."

"She did so well because I taught her the value of hard work."

"It was my revision techniques that helped him secure those grades."

People remark how proud we must be of these accomplishments and this admiration creates fuel for us.

How many times do you hear of certain people accused of plagiarism? They took a particular riff from a less well-known song and turned it into a huge hit? An idea for a screenplay was purloined by a famous director and became box office gold? That is our kind at work. Once we have rightly taken our place in the stratosphere of the special it becomes easier to steal the credit. People less well known will appear with their ideas and suggestions and offer them to us for consideration. We will reject them and then use them ourselves but pass them off as our creation. Try and sue us and we will mobilise our resources to head you off at the pass. We will deploy our manipulative skills to ensure you are regarding as a troublemaker. You have been stalking us and are no more than an obsessive fan. You pinched the idea from us and then tried to make out that it was yours.

Taking the credit for your ideas works best for us in the world of work and business because there are more people who will then praise us for our false achievement. This greater number of admirers gives us more fuel and makes us feel more powerful. It also helps to support our carefully constructed persona of successful businessman, talented musician or outstanding artist. This need for repeated admiration will bleed into our home lives as well. Should you select a gift for a family member, by way of example, which exhibits that some care and thought has gone into it, when that person opens it and declares their surprise and thanks we will step in and tell them how hard we look for it so that their thanks and admiration shines on to us. If you dare to contradict us by pointing out that it was you who selected, the gift (and since when did we ever bother to think about buying anybody else something?) then expect to be attacked. Our behaviour in this regard can be regarded as petty. We return home to see that you have spent the entire day painting the living room.

"It was a good colour I picked, wasn't it?" I will remark without any hint of shame as we ignore your hard work and seek to steal the credit for a job well done. If one of our children has done a good job cleaning the car and you make mention of this, I will dive in by stating,

"Yes but I showed her what to do."

Not only must I claim credit for anything and everything, nobody else is allowed a look in. The spotlight of congratulation cannot ever shine on anyone but me. Do not expect to be thanked or given praise for what you do for us or around our home. I expect you to do this and after all, I earn the money that pays the mortgage so the least you can do is run a decent home in return. This repeated need to seize the glory and deny you even a modicum of thanks and credit becomes infuriating and underlines our child-like need for repeated praise and admiration.

39. Why are you in such a rush to secure our commitment to you? Why do you want to get married or move in so soon with us? (From Stephanie)

Our purpose in life is to extract fuel from you. In order to achieve this sole aim, we need you around us and committed to us so that our source of fuel is almost always present. We do not need to be physically with you to achieve this. The readiness of technology to enable us to remain in contact with you through a plethora of methods satisfies this desire for often and repeated contact. What we need to achieve is that you feel compelled to interact with us. You must feel obliged to spend time with us, answer out telephone call and/or respond to our text messages. Part of this is achieved by flattery as described in the previous chapter. When we send you a compliment in a text you, being a decent and well-mannered person will answer it. Often you will write back conveying your thanks and also sending a compliment to us as well. This provides us with what we want. Your attention and admiration.

We need this obligation to become deeper however. We not only want you to respond when we get in touch with you, we also want you to contact us irrespective of our approach to you. We want you to think of us from the moment you wake up so that you call us. We require you to have us in our thoughts so that you will provide us with the attention that we crave.

Unlike a normal, healthy relationship which develops over time at a sensible pace which is acceptable to both people, we want to rush you into commitment. We want you attached to us a soon as possible so that you are beholden to our demands and thus you feel obligated to do what we want. If you have a serious commitment to us, we know, because you are that decent and honest person that you will not renege on your obligations. You will get in touch to ask how we are, you will follow us from room to room to ascertain what is wrong when we subject you to a bout of silent treatment and you will do your utmost to keep us happy. We know you will do this because we recognise that as an empathic individual you take your responsibilities seriously and adhere to them. As part of a couple, you will look to maintain that state of affairs by doing anything and everything possible to ensure that we do not break up. This means that you will bend over backwards to facilitate us. Even in a normal relationship the split between two people is rarely an even fifty per cent each. Often one person does more for the other and sometimes this percentage vacillates dependent on the particular strand of the relationship. On the one hand, one person may contribute more financially than their partner but then that person provides more in terms of handling the household's administrative affairs. There is nothing wrong with one person giving more than the other in a relationship. In relationships involving my kind and me however that percentage is so heavily skewed in our favour, across all elements of the relationship that is bordering on indentured servitude. It has to be this way in order for us to extract the fuel we need. We do not like to expend our own energy in maintaining the relationship. We prefer to use it to acquire more fuel, either by hunting out new sources of supply or by unleashing our wide variety of manipulative wiles against you. Thus, in order to conserve our fuel for our malign purposes, it falls to you to expend your energies in the upkeep of our relationship.

The extent and degree by which we require you to give your all, often for little in return, means that in the early stages of a relationship most people would regard that as wrong and seek to remove themselves from this unpleasant position. We cannot have you do that. We will use flattery to keep you where we want you but we are unable to maintain this for too long as it will take up too much of our energies. Accordingly, we need to make you commit to us in some other form. This means we will look to achieve one of the following:

1. Move in together (usually we prefer to move into your home whilst keeping our own property as a bolt hole which we can remove ourselves to when we are subjecting you to silent treatment. Also, we like to move into your property as this enables us to argue that you should shoulder the bills, since after all, it is *your* house.)

2. Get engaged and married; and/or

3. Get you pregnant or become pregnant

By achieving one or all of these situations we are able to bind you to us. You will think that this is wonderful. We are evidently so in love with you that we want to take such a major step with you. It has nothing to do with love, it is all about ensuring that you are committed to us and thus in the best possible position to provide us with fuel. By bringing about these scenarios you are less likely to leave and more likely to want to keep trying to please us, even when we are subjecting you to awful devaluation. You do not want to give up since you are, for example, a firm believer in the institution of marriage. You try to keep us together because your parents have always been together and you always swore you would do the same. You want to overcome the problems (always caused by us, not you, despite what we keep telling you) because we have children together and you do not want them to come from a broken home. All your ingrained values are the methods by which we know that you will not shirk your responsibilities and by which you will remain committed to us.

It also provides the means by which we can seek to hoover you back in at a later stage after we have discarded you but decide we want to, we have to, extract some further fuel from you. Consider these statements: -

"I decided to give her a further chance; she is still my wife after all."

"I know what he did was wrong but he said he is sorry and he wants to be there for our children. I cannot deny them that can I?"

"He cannot go back to that dingy apartment and be on his own. I don't like to think of him sat alone, not when it is clear there is something wrong. This is our home and he should be here."

Any of those sound familiar?

We will move at light speed to bring about this level of commitment. We make you think that this is the ultimate in showing our commitment to you. That is wrong. It is all about making your committed to us. We do not recognise that we have any obligation to you at all. Nobody can know one another well enough to marry after six weeks. What trials and tribulations have you experienced together to ensure that you are compatible? What situations have you seen one another in to know that your relationship can endure the slings and arrows that life will send your way? We however will blind you to all of this with our campaign of love bombing so that you will seize this chance to bond with us in the ultimate fashion, in an instant. You will not want to lose somebody as wonderful as us, someone who has treated you better and more wonderfully than anyone else. You will do anything to keep us and the fact that we have suggested that we move in together has made your dreams come true. He must feel the way I do if he is proposing so soon, mustn't he?

Once the commitment has been achieved you will see our behaviour towards you alter. Sometimes it is almost other night, sometimes it is months, maybe if you are really lucky (or is that unlucky) it will be a few years, but that change will come. The fact we have secured your commitment provides us with carte blanche to do as we please and you will put up with it. In fact, the existence of this commitment means that you will allow yourself to be subjected to the very worst of our behaviour and you will work harder to try and make things right.

The knock-out blow in terms of securing commitment is to have children with you. This is a very powerful method of ensuring we get what we want. Not only will you be loath to have the relationship end, for the sake of the children, should you muster sufficient strength and willpower to escape us, the fact we will still be able to see the children means you can never be truly free of our influence. We will have a conduit by which we can continue to exert our behaviours over you and extract fuel from you. This may be by virtue of contact with you (speaking on the telephone about arrangements concerning the children or attending in person to collect or drop them off). It may also be by using the children as a method by which we triangulate with you. We secure their affections by denigrating you and thus prompting you to react when the children repeat our lies about you. Your only hope is that eventually the children see through our façade and decide they do not want to have anything to do with us. That is unlikely to happen (if at all) for a number of years. You also run the real risk that our behaviours will have created another version of ourselves in one of our children and thus the nightmare will be propagated.

40. Can you be friends with your narcissist following a relationship with one? Under what terms after a relationship? (From Shivali)

We would have no hesitation at all remaining friends with you following the cessation of an intimate relationship. This would prove advantageous to us because: -

1. You would continue to provide fuel as a high-ranking secondary source of fuel;

2. You would save us the need to undertake a hoover. Although the fuel from a hoover is always desirable, we would be content with the fact that you are providing us with fuel from the position as a friend, for a period of time at least.

3. Dependent on our arrangements with a new primary source of fuel, we may have cause to hoover you. Not to provide fuel, since you would already be doing this in the context of the friendship, but in order to bring you back into the fold as an intimate partner whereupon we would receive fuel arising from the hoover and thereafter from the provision of your positive fuel as the reinstated partner.

4. Even if we decided against hoovering you, you would make yourself readily available as someone with whom we could triangulate our new partner.

5. If we discarded you, if you decided you want to remain friends with us we would most likely resist it at first so as to draw negative fuel from you. You would keep hanging on in order to remain friends and you would react to our Malign Follow-Up Hoovers. You would be making life easier for us.

6. If you decided to end the intimate relationship but you have not instigated no contact and instead have decided to stay in touch with us as friends, we will welcome this for the fuel provided and the potential ease by which we

can use you for triangulation and the potential hoover for both negative fuel and to bring you back in to our grip as an intimate partner.

It does rather beg the question why you would want to be remain friends with somebody who has abused you but it may be the case that the effect of ever presence is proving too difficult for you to handle and you wish to remain in contact, notwithstanding the risk it presents to you.

41. Are you really happy/in love with the new target? (From So Sad)

We are no more in love with the new prospect that we were with you. What we are in love with is their fuel. It is better, stronger and more potent than what you provided. You let us down. Your replacement is superior and we question why on earth we chose you. In fact, you ensnared us and we tried to help you deal with your problems. We realized that you had issues but being the kind and pleasant people that we are, we tried to help you and provided you with support, money, accommodation and so much more. Of course you threw it all back in our faces, abused us, mistreated us and left us confused and bewildered. Thank goodness we found the new prospect. He or she truly understands us, makes us feel complete, we are soulmates, we were always destined to be together. I do not understand what I saw in you at all. In fact, I was obviously conned by you and you took advantage of me in a moment of weakness. I still do not understand why you did as you did, after everything that I had done for you and perhaps I will never know. Feel free to look at all the pictures of me and the new prospect which I have plastered all over Facebook whilst deleting anything to do with you. I am so much happier now I am with her/him. This is the one.

Sound familiar? Was this all said to you about the person you replaced? The simple fact is that because we always win we are always able to revise history. Once upon a time you were placed on a pedestal and we broadcast to the world how much we adored you and that we wanted to be with you forever. Suddenly you became a pariah and hated. The exact same fate awaits your replacement. We hope that it will not happen. We hope that this time we have selected somebody that will keep supplying us with the positive fuel so that there is no fall from grace but it has never happened so far and therefore the likelihood of it happening in the future is pretty remote. Of course we appear happy with our new prospect because we are. We have something new and shiny which does as it is told and is caught in the full glare of our charm headlights. Not like you, the person who became clingy and disappointing, providing us with aggravation, questions and calls to account. By comparison this person is wonderful. We automatically forget how wonderful everything was with you in the beginning, until we decide to reinstate that golden period when we hoover you. For now, we want you to feel dejected and miserable as you look on and observe us smiling and content, parading our new acquisition around to everybody (just as we did with you). The person may change but the behaviors are the same for her as they were for you as they were for the ten other people before you.

We want to make you jealous. We want to upset you. You want you to try and contact us and provide us with negative fuel as you wail and whine. This powers our seduction of the new person as we look on in disgust at you and with rapt admiration at our new find. We truly believe they are better than you, although in reality, there may be no difference. You are often left wondering whether we are happy with this new person and why cannot it be you? What have they done which has succeeded where you failed? What if this state of affairs lasts forever and we both live happily ever after as you look on bitter and twisted? That is what we want you to think. We want you this way so we can draw negative fuel from you and then hoover you at a later stage. The reality is that what you see is just as much an illusion as it was with you and it will all come tumbling down soon enough. It is hard to believe and hard to take when you see it being played out in front of you, but that is the reality of the situation. You should take solace from the fact that what you went through will happen to your replacement even though we will repeatedly hope this is not the case and we will often tell you how much better than you this new person is. It is all designed to grind you down and provoke you into providing us fuel. Many people find this situation difficult to deal with because they take it at face value and think that they must have done something wrong if we are now happy with someone else. That is the result of the manipulative behavior which we apply against you. By wearing you down we have you thinking that you are at fault and this then colours your view when you see us with somebody else. You assume that they know something you do not, that they have done something better and that they will get the golden period which you still want. This is actually a powerful incentive we use to make you susceptible to the hoover and you are being triangulated by us before you know it. It is all part of the illusion.

42. Is the reason you start to find things we do wrong simply because you are getting too close and you are afraid of being hurt or abandoned and this is your way of protecting yourself? (From Fool Me)

We do not feel close to you. We feel close to your fuel and that is what is the key determinant in our change of behaviour towards you. When we seduce you, you are interesting, fascinating and wonderful. We truly see great things for us both. Your praise, admiration and love are unlike anything we have experienced before (since we so conveniently erase everyone else that came before) and we reciprocate this. The difference is, is that your love and admiration, your compliments and your praise are all genuine. Ours are not. The fuel that you provide us during the seduction and the golden period is fresh, potent and there is a lot of it. Then something changes. You do not sustain the level of positive fuel that we are used to or that we need. You do not provide it with the same potency and this let us down. By failing in the sole role that we have identified you (over so many other people) for, you have let us down badly. In fact, you are inherently criticizing us. You are suggesting that we are no longer worth providing this fuel for. You are telling us that we are not worth giving the time, attention and compliments etc. that you once did. You of course respond by telling us that you love us just as much but that, well, things have become more settled and you show your love for us in a different, more deep-seated way. That may well be the case from your perspective but that is no good to us. From our perspective you are not giving us the fuel that we need and the fuel that you are obliged to do so. You are criticising us. This results in our fury igniting and then we lash out at you. You are a failure and the love-bombing and the golden period ends just like that. There is no warning and no explanation.

We then find fault with everything you do (even when viewed from your perspective you have not done anything wrong) because we have to. We have to do this to recover negative fuel from you. This is now even more potent because it contrasts with the positive fuel and the ease by which we obtained it from you. Negative fuel is harder to extract because it goes contrary to the way you wish to behave and therefore once we obtain it, it tastes all the sweeter and more potent. Of course, with an intimate partner who is a primary source we are only able to do this following your seduction. You cause us to have to find fault with you. In a way it is a self-defence mechanism. It is not one activated by concerns that we are becoming too close to you. That does not happen because we are constructed in a different way to you. The self-defence mechanism operates as means to ensure that we receive the fuel we need to preserve out existence at the strength, potency and volume that is appropriate. Thus, when you let us down, we switch to devaluing you as a means of ensuring we receive fuel from you.

43. How do narcissists learn or come about the ability to completely twist or modify the truth? My mind cannot even comprehend this ability nor can it think that fast! (From Jennifer)

The truth is an elastic concept and one which we are entirely content to stretch and snap to suit our purposes. There are two fundamental reasons why we twist the truth:
-

1. To draw fuel from you by reason of your reaction when we twist the truth; and
2. To confuse you so you remain under out control.

I have explained above why we lie so much, so in this answer I have seized on Jennifer's use of twisting the truth to address the concept of blame-shifting. We are never wrong. We are never to blame. We are not accountable to anybody for what we say or do because we are entitled to do as we please, we are superior and we do not recognize boundaries.

Projection is where we project our wrong behaviours on to you and accuse you of carrying them out. Blame-shifting is where we move the blame on to you or somebody else but never allow it to remain with us. This is one of the reasons why we twist the truth. We may allow the essential facts to remain. Indeed, if we do not have to challenge those facts so much the better as this will save our energy. Instead, what we do is use those same facts but twist them in order to apportion the blame elsewhere. At its simplest an example would be where we have arrived home late from the bar because we have been flirting with other women as part of the seduction of someone else as we wish to tee up a replacement for you. The conversation may go something like this, with you starting it.

"You are home late, where have you been?"

"Yes it is late." (We are not disputing the facts)

"So where have you been? The bar."

"I don't know why you are asking me that. You know I was at the bar. I told you that." (Not disputing the facts but raising the point that you are asking pointless questions and insinuating you are doing so because you have an agenda).

"So why are you so late then?"

"I was talking to some people." (Not a lie.)

"Huh, I bet you were, no doubt some cheap whores, I can smell their perfume on you."

"Well they were wearing a lot I must admit and I was stood next to them." (Again not disputing the facts)

"You've been flirting on again I bet, that is why you come in at this time."

"How would you know; you were not there." (Undeniable fact).

"I don't need to be there to know it."

"Oh I see, so you just make assumptions based on something you have not seen, that's really fair of you isn't it?"

"I don't need to be there to know."

"Is that right? Well, how many men have you been servicing here since I have been out talking to people in the bar?"

"What are you talking about? I haven't been doing anything, I have been sat here on my own watching television."

"So you say, but I say you have been entertaining men behind my back."

"Nonsense."

"Well according to you I don't have to see it to accuse you of it so that's what I say you have been doing."

"That's just ridiculous."

"Well that must mean your accusation about me, based on nothing, based on not being there, when I was there and all I was doing was giving some advice to a friend of the bar man who wanted some advice concerning a neighbor problem that she is having, is ridiculous." (Blame being shifted)

"That's different. I know what you have been doing."

"Really how? You weren't there."

"I don't need to be there. I can just tell."

"Telepathic are we now. Got a sixth sense. You want to watch your tongue, making things up about me when you have no basis for doing so. I was out speaking to some people and you behave like this when I come in. Is it any wonder I want to go out? You always do this when I want to enjoy myself, I am helping someone and you jump to conclusions based on nothing. I am sick of you treating me this way."

On it goes as the blame for being out late is taken away from me and pinned on you as the blame for being a hectoring and nagging partner.

Most of what was said there was true but it was twisted in order to deflect the attack from us and to make you look bad so we could provoke a reaction from you as you became frustrated, angry or upset and thus we gain fuel. We twist the truth in a subtle manner so we can assert we are being acceptably evasive and preventing you from gaining the upper hand in any way.

44. Why can't there be a finite termination to the relationship with a goal to try to end things peacefully and take away the good things you enjoyed about each other – then be done for good? Why can't the good transcend all the nastiness? (From MLA)

People do often wonder why it is necessary to keep on in a savage and nasty way with somebody when the relationship has ended. Those intentions, noble as they might be, may apply to normal and well-adjusted people who have ended a relationship but they are not applicable to us. The reasons why this cannot happen are as follows: -

1. If we discarded you then we saw no further worth in retaining you. Accordingly, you have been cast aside. We have no interest in being pleasant with you. We regard you as a faulty appliance. We cannot carry a faulty appliance around as we need a functioning one so you are cast to one side. There is no point remaining on good terms as this serves no purpose to us because why would we want any contact with you when we are busy with our new primary source? We will want contact with you at a later stage when we hoover and we will try to draw you back in and if that fails take the negative fuel through Malign Follow-Up Hoovers because we need the fuel;

2. If you ended the relationship and tried to do so in an amicable fashion by taking the good things away from it as a lasting memory, this is not good to us. You have stopped our fuel supply. You have criticized us. This injury transcends any notion of parting on the basis that is suggested. We have no option other than to hoover you or go elsewhere. You have wounded us and therefore we cannot and will not part on the terms suggested.

3. You are just as to blame as well. The abuse you have suffered causes you to depart often on terms which contravene those suggested in the question above.

This is somewhat understandable. Why would you want everything to be sweetness and light when you have been treated in this fashion?

4. Relationships with us do not just fizzle out. You are either discarded or you try to escape us with the predictable reaction from us. Even if we are a low-functioning narcissist who had an alternative primary source ready, thus removing the need for an Initial Grand Hoover, we would still look to do Follow-Up Hoovers if you came within our sphere of influence or we would just forget about you as we jettison the memory of you as we do and focus on our new supply instead. There is nothing to be gained by walking away with happy memories of what once was.

5. We delete these memories save for when we want to hoover, so we have no interest in parting on such terms.

6. The goodness that occurred is viewed once again from your perspective. To us it was about getting fuel. You gave great fuel and then you did not. All we now remember is the latter. The former may as well have never existed.

Accordingly, the way that we are created and the demands placed on us by fuel mean that there can never be a parting of the ways where the good memories prevail and the parting is amicable.

45. Do you realise that your destruction of our souls, in a high percentage of us, does eventually raise our vibration and lead to our soul awakening which transforms our entire existence to one of bliss? How does this make you feel? Are you angered by it? Do you disbelieve it? Does it make you feel even more superior? Are you resentful? Are you even aware of this? (From Carole)

No I did not realise that. I have not had anybody else every tell me that. If someone that I discarded told me that then I would regard that as a challenge and commence a hoover in order to suck them back in by inviting them to show me how this bliss manifested, whether they might share it with me and allow me to experience such a transformation too. I would feign amazement at how this happens and would ask to be granted the same experience too so that together we could transcend to a higher state of consciousness. I would invite this person to do this in order to help and heal me. By adopting their belief, I would bring them back under my control and then recommence the narcissistic cycle.

If I was told all of this but the person resisted the hoover as described above, then I would switch to a malign stance and utilize this supposed bliss as a method of drawing negative fuel from the person.

In terms of how it makes me feel, I am more concerned about regaining fuel as opposed to whether you are in a state of bliss or not. Your state of bliss does not affect my condition of superiority. In fact, your state post discard or post escape whether it is happiness, sadness, regret, bliss or otherwise just becomes the conduit and mechanism by which I shall look to hoover. What affects me is the loss of fuel and the need to reinstate that either as a positive outcome from an Initial Grand Hoover or as a negative outcome from a Malign Follow Up Hoover. You can achieve any state you want so long as you give me fuel.

46. Was any of the golden period real? Even part of it? (From PT)

In a word, no. The golden period was all an illusion. It is something that many people fail to grasp and something they never end up accepting. This is understandable. The victim will have given their love in many ways and since their love was genuine they cannot believe that somebody else could fabricate what we showed. It seemed so genuine that it beggars belief that it could all be false. The victim cannot accept that he or she has been hoodwinked to such a degree and therefore scrambles desperately for answers in order to try to gain some sense of reason and understanding. They want some confirmation that they were not totally duped but that is what has happened. The illusion of the golden period is probably the most powerful weapon that our kind deploys against you. It is powerful because: -

1. It draws you to us;
2. It causes you to miss red flags or not pay attention to them;
3. It causes you to provide significant and potent positive fuel;
4. It binds you to us;
5. It keeps you clinging on when we abuse you because you want the golden period back and you believe you can attain that;
6. It is used to prevent you leaving us;
7. It forms the basis of a hoover when we discard you;
8. It forms the basis of a hoover when you try and escape us
9. It causes you to keep thinking it was real for a long time (perhaps always) afterwards so you never truly move on from us.

That is how powerful it is.

When we cast you aside in our callous manner and leave you despairing and devastated in the dirt, the smouldering ruins of the fabricated world now laid bare and razed to the ground, all around you, you will spend many hours dissecting, analysing and reviewing what has happened. The questions that form as a consequence of our magnificent seduction, our brutal abuse and our reckless discard come thick, fast and often. Did he love me? How could he have treated me this way? How did the happiness turn so sour and so quickly? Is he with someone else? How will he treat her? What if she makes him happy? How could he treat me like this after everything that I have done? How does he sleep at night? How can he look at himself in the mirror? Has he done this to other people? Maybe his ex-wife was right about him and tried to warn me? Did I do something wrong? Did I bring it on myself? What if I had tried harder to please him? Why did he not say he was unhappy with me, I would have done something about it? Why won't he speak to me? Will I ever see him again? What have I done to deserve this? Was he every happy? Why was he so angry? Surely he meant some of it?

This last question is the refuge of the deluded. A place where you attempt to gain some solace and relief from the wounds that you still bear after becoming entangled with us. You look to any shred that may give you some comfort from the hurt, some piece of the jigsaw that will make everything click into place and some consolation that he really did love something about you and he showed that to you. You might seize upon all those times you and I attended those classical music concerts, when we sat holding hands and listen to the philharmonic orchestra as they played Rimsky-Korsakov's Scherezade. You remember looking across and smiling at how content I looked. I certainly seemed to be enjoying the performance and indeed I spoke about it in glowing terms in the bar afterwards. I may have enjoyed the performance and appreciated the skill and dedication of the musicians but I enjoyed more making you think that this was something I really enjoyed so that you poured admiration and positive fuel my way.

How about the excitement I exhibited when you organised for us to attend a wine tasting course led by that television personality? That must have been true appreciation of what you had organised for me. I appreciated how you had committed such a loving gesture and fuelled me as I became excited at the prospect of showing off in front of the other attendees about my knowledge of wine and outshining the personality. That is what motivated me. You look back through the love letters, the elegant copper plate handwriting which conveyed such deep and heartfelt emotions. The words were so moving and now as you re-read them the tears form in your eyes as the memory of hearing me reading to them cuts through you. Surely I must have meant those words, they are so passionate and meaningful. I meant those words as a way to gain more fuel from you, to make you want me all the more and your tearful appreciation made me feel powerful and fuelled as I read to you. You recall your favourite restaurant and the numerous times that I took you there. Surely I enjoyed that? I always complimented the chef and on several times I booked it as a surprise. I found the food mediocre but your reaction to knowing that you were going there and your gushing appreciation when we dined at this restaurant meant that enduring the bland cuisine and irritating maitre'd was entirely worth it. How about then the times we danced cheek to cheek to Sade or Dido. You felt so close to me then and hadn't I said that I felt as if time had stood still and the rest of the world had melted away. Surely I must have meant that? Not so, I hated those artists and I wiled away the tedious minutes drinking in your fuel and plotting my further machinations. There are occasions when we do certain things for you, or behave in a certain way, or do things with you which may coincide with things that we like. I will admit that, but to say that we loved them and to say that we loved them because of you is erroneous. What we loved more than anything was the fuel that you provided to us as a consequence of your reaction to dining at that restaurant, or dancing cheek to cheek or attending the basketball together. The outings with friends, the gardening together, the sex, the holding hands, the playing of computer games, the films, the television shows and on and on, all of it was love because of the fuel you gave when we did those things together and you deemed them to be special. It was the fuel. You may delude yourself and feel free to do so, it will just make hoovering you at a later stage easier. Convince yourself some of it was real. Convince yourself that some of it was worthwhile and not wasted. That is your choice and once which makes you all the more susceptible to me sinking my teeth into you again and drawing yet more fuel from you. So, when you ask yourself yet again that surely he meant some of it when I did as I did and said as I said, you know the answer is that the only thing I meant was that I loved the fuel you gave me.

47. Can there ever be a working long-term relationship with one of your kind? (From TCT)

The answer is yes, although this comes with the caveat that it depends on what you understand by the word "working". From our perspective we regard it as a relationship in perpetuity once you have been targeted by us. We will look to draw fuel from you until we shuffle off this mortal coil. From the instant that we target you through seduction all the way to the repeated hoovers which will follow discard and/or your attempts to escape we consider our relationship with you to be one which will always last and one which works in terms of you providing us with fuel. If you place yourself within our sphere of influence, then we will hoover you time and time again. We do not care how you feel about this arrangement. This is what we want and need.

From your perspective one would imagine that by a working relationship you mean one that operates in the same way as one which normal and well-adjusted people have. That just does not and will not happen with our kind. Our need for fuel means that we follow the cycle of seduce, devalue, discard and hoover which means you will be placed on a rollercoaster for as long as you interact with us.

Is there another way? If you chose to remain with us, then you would be committing yourself to trying to provide us with positive fuel throughout in order to avoid the devaluation and discard. So far, nobody I have coupled with has been able to achieve this. That does not mean that I have given up the prospect of it ever happening, but the prospects admittedly, based on past experiences do not look good. It would require you to ensure that the fuel you provide is as potent as it was on day one of our coupling. It is questionable whether you are able to do this. If somehow you are then there would be no need for the devaluation and discard and there will be a continuation of the golden period. This would be the ideal state for both parties, but as I have mentioned, it has never happened yet and I suspect it just cannot because you are not equal to the task of providing the fuel at the required level forever.

Since that state of nirvana is most unlikely to be achieved then the devaluation will follow. Might you continue a working relationship with your narcissist notwithstanding this? Potentially yes. You would have to keep providing the negative fuel and this means you would be subjected to sustained and prolonged abuse. You are not superhuman and therefore this will take its toll on you. You may certainly find ways to manage the abuse so it is less damaging to you, if you decide to remain within the relationship and **Escape** provides information on doing so, enabling you to escape the worst of our behaviours. You may be able to survive the devaluation by reducing the effect whilst still providing the negative fuel and ensuring that when there is a respite period you pump out fantastic positive fuel again. You could learn to live with the narcissist but all the compromises would be coming from you. You would need to adapt the way you behaved to accommodate his or her demands, attend to them, manage him or her so the vitriol is not as caustic when applied to you. You would have to forgo much of what makes you, you in order to fit in around the whims and behaviours of your narcissist.

You will in all likelihood be discarded and you will have to manage that also. You would have to tolerate infidelity as he or she seeks out another primary source and await the hoover, which will come. You could adopt a stance of always submitting to the hoover and pouring with positive hoover fuel so you know that your narcissist will always return to you, but you would have to do this in the knowledge that he or she has been somewhere else, with someone else and this will happen again. You will no doubt find it hard when discarded and learning that he or she is with someone else not to worry that this time it is over and her or she is not coming back. This will put you on edge and create anxiety.

You also have to ask yourself what would you get out of this? We get the fuel. You manage to handle the worst of our behaviours, dampening them down and by understanding what is happening and what happens this will reduce some of your concerns, but ultimately, to someone like you who is a love devotee and empathic, can it be said that operating in this way is really how you would want to live your life? It would be great for us knowing that you will never go no contact, that you will always strive to provide fuel both positive and negative, that you will always be ready to be hoovered and you will accept our behaviours. This is almost ideal for us, but would it really work for you.

It you are prepared to make massive compromises to your life and dignity, you may achieve something which might be regarded as a working relationship with your narcissist. There will be good moments when the golden period is extended and when it returns during respite periods and hoovers but ultimately it will be one-sided.

48. Why is negative fuel more satisfying than positive fuel? (From TCT)

This is correct as a general proposition but the relationship between the two requires further examination. Readers of **Fuel** will be familiar with the fuel index. This is the dynamic between the proximity of supply (the type of appliance supplying the fuel) and the method of delivery (whether the fuel comes as words or gestures, whether they are admiring, loving, angry or tearful). The fuel from a remote stranger is generally weaker than that from an intimate partner, hence why intimate partners are chosen nearly exclusively for the position of primary source to us. Accordingly, if an intimate partner provides us with admiring words that amounst to a significant and high dose of fuel in accordance with the fuel index. Ordinarily, negative reactions (words or gestures) outrank those of a positive nature. However, an intimate partner providing us with admiring words far outweighs a remote stranger providing us with tearful words, even though tearful words are the highest form of method of delivery. Thus, when considering the relationship between negative fuel and positive fuel it is correct to say that negative responses outrank positive ones in the method of delivery. However, this cannot be regarded in isolation as the fuel arises from a proximity of supply as well and that must always be considered too. There are, therefore, instances where positive responses (because of the nature of the provider) will outrank negative responses (again because of the nature of the provider).

If, however the provider is the same, say a family member, then a negative reaction from this family member will always provide fuel that is more potent than the same family member providing a positive reaction. Accordingly, the question really is, why are negative **reactions** viewed as more potent than positive **reactions**?

The answer to this is straightforward. It is easier to cause somebody to be positive. Nearly all people prefer to provide positive reactions. It is easier and regarded as more socially acceptable to provide these positive reactions and therefore it is not particularly difficult to cause them in people. Negative reactions are, as a rule, harder to draw from people. People try to stay cheerful rather than respond in a sad fashion. People try to keep their tempers and their hatred under control before erupting. Accordingly, drawing a negative reaction is harder but this makes it all the more satisfying for us. This effect is heightened by the nature of our usual victims. The empaths, super empaths and co-dependents are believers in honesty, love and decency. They want to heal people, to see the best in them and help. They exhibit patience and understanding and prefer to deal in the realm of positivity. This means it is even harder to than when dealing with a normal person to draw a negative reaction from an empath (that is until they become ground down by the abuse) and accordingly they have an innate resistance which we must overcome by the application of various tools from our devil's toolkit. Drawing these negative reactions from empathic individuals is even more satisfying and that is why the negative reaction ranks higher and subject to who is providing that reaction, the fuel will be more potent.

It is worth adding that in order to draw negative fuel from the higher ranking proximities of supply then there must be a postivie relationship beforehand. One may be able to draw negative fuel from a waitress (minion) by criticising her dilatory serving response without having paid her a compliemtn beforehand, but with the higher ranking proximities of supply it is necessary to establish positive fuel first. Trying to draw negative fuel from the off will not work. The subject is unlikely to respond (because there has to have been the positivity there first to accentuate the nature of our behaviour to cause the negative fuel to be provided) and if they happened to, in a rare instance, the subject would move quickly away from us because they have not been bound to us by the seduction period. It accordingly means that with the higher ranking proximities of supply that we must seduce them, draw positive fuel for a period of time because we can then switch to the more potent negative reactions and the commensurate negative fuel that arises.

49. Do you ever actually consider a valued source a true friend? (From Hope)

No. We regard that person as a true and valued appliance because all we are interested in is the fuel that is provided. If we happen to share similar interests, enjoy conversing with this person and find them amusing that is just a fortunate coincidence. Those are not the reasons why we chose this person and became a friend with him or her. This person was chosen primarily for their ability to provide us with fuel, but also their ability to provide us with traits that we can take for ourselves and also for their loyalty in being a member of my coterie or even a Lieutenant. This means that when we assess somebody and decide they should be an Outer or Inner Circle Friend we look at: -

1. Fuel provision;
2. Traits; and
3. Loyalty.

Those are what matter to us. If there are other matters associated with this person which are acceptable then that is a coincidence. A friend may remain one of our secondary sources for a considerable period of time if they function in that role effectively. There is less need to subject a secondary source to devaluation (unlike the primary source) and accordingly if they remain a functioning and valued appliance they can remain with us as friends for some time. We have little need to discard them. Often (although not always) the friend realizes that they are being used and invariably drifts away from us. We may consider applying a hoover if they have something that we need or we regard them as troublemaker and decide they must be punished, otherwise we will just cut them adrift, bad mouth them to other people and find a replacement. We find making new friends extremely easy.

It is rare to find that we have long-standing friends although once in a while it can happen. Those people are completely brainwashed to our ways and will be a

Lieutenant who will show unflinching loyalty to us. Alternatively, the friend will drift in and out, functioning appropriately as an outer circle friend but doing no more, so they do not merit promotion but there is no need to devalue and discard them.

50. If you want to keep a good source in reserve why discard so badly why not give them closure and downgrade to friend status? (From Freedom)

The clue to the answer to this question lies in the comment about "a good source". The reason we discard you is because you are no longer a good source. This state of affairs arises because: -

1. You are not providing the negative fuel at the level we require during our continuing devaluation of you. This may be because you are working us out and whilst not able to escape us by going no contact you are applying principles which diminish the provision of negative reactions and thus we are not obtaining the relevant negative fuel from you. Alternatively, you are pushed to a place where you are barely functioning and therefore you are not responding as you have become numb.

2. The new prospect is providing excellent positive fuel and we decide to concentrate on this as our primary source now, meaning you are no longer required.

Since you are no longer a good source (either through production and/or comparison) we discard you. We do not downgrade you because we want to keep your status as an intimate partner for the forthcoming hoover. The fuel we get from you as a former intimate partner is excellent when we hoover you. Far better to do obtain it from you as a former intimate partner than as a friend. We also take the view that our hoover will be more likely to succeed when premised on returning to an intimate relationship with you rather than as a friend.

The discard has to be harsh for several reasons: -

1. Punishment for you failing us as a good source of fuel;

2. To maintain your hurt so negative fuel can be drawn again at some point;

3. To maintain your confusion so you are more susceptible to a hoover at a later stage.

Dropping you gently would serve no purpose to us and it is all about us. Not about oyu. We do not allow closure. This is because our relationship with you is one of perpetuity. We never want to let you escape us. Ever.

Further required reading from H G Tudor

Evil

Narcissist: Seduction

Narcissist: Ensnared

Manipulated

Confessions of a Narcissist

More Confessions of a Narcissist

Further Confessions of a Narcissist

From the Mouth of a Narcissist

Escape: How to Beat the Narcissist

Danger: 50 Things You Should Not Do with a Narcissist

Departure Imminent: Preparing for No Contact to beat the Narcissist

Fuel

Chained: The Narcissist's Co-Dependent

A Delinquent Mind

Fury

Beautiful and Barbaric

The Devil's Toolkit

Sex and the Narcissist

Treasured and Tormented

No Contact: How to Beat the Narcissist

Revenge: How to Beat the Narcissist

Adored and Abhorred

Sitting Target: How and Why the Narcissist Chooses You

Black Hole: The Narcissistic Hoover

A Grimoire of Narcissism

Cherished and Chastised

Red Flag: 50 Warning Signs of Narcissistic Seduction

All available on Amazon

Further interaction with H G Tudor

Knowing the Narcissist

@narcissist_me

Facebook

Narcsite.wordpress.com

CPSIA information can be obtained
at www.ICGtesting.com
Printed in the USA
LVOW13s1004290117
522507LV00027B/788/P